We Enjoyed Alaska — But Russell Just About Killed Us!

Copyright © 2008, 2009 by Julian Anderson Williams, all rights reserved. No part of this book may be reproduced, stored or transmitted in any form, by any means, without written permission from Julian Anderson Williams and/or ThomasMax Publishing. An exception is made for brief excerpts and passages used for review purposes.

This book is a collection of articles originally published in *The Douglas Enterprise*. The first article appeared Aug. 6, 2008, titled *Old Jacksonville, GA, Made Me Want To See Alaska (Part One)*. The series, presented in its entirety in this book, was published in 51 parts in the newspaper, the final part appearing on Sept. 2, 2009.

Cover design by ThomasMax (Lee Clevenger & R. Preston Ward)

ISBN-13: 978-0-9842626-1-8
ISBN-10: 0-9842626-1-x

First Printing, December 2009

Published by:

ThomasMax Publishing
P.O. Box 250054
Atlanta, GA 30325
www.thomasmax.com

*I dedicate this book to my wife, Joanne,
who supported and helped me in this effort.*

*Also, to Russell,
who "explained the other side" of Alaska.*

Table of Contents

Part 1 - Crying Time And Leaving Georgia For Icebergs
Part 2 - We Needed General Breckinridge And Jesse James In Our Bus Restroom
Part 3 - Restroom Extrication, Breckinridge's Relatives And The Corn Palace
Part 4 - Stuffed Horses, Old Schoolhouses And The Badlands
Part 5 - Old Jacksonville, Ga. And Murdo, South Dakota Had Connections
Part 6 - Found Free Ice Water Before Seeing Mount Rushmore
Part 7 - Sundance Kid And General Custer Met Us Down The Road
Part 8 - Little Bighorn Did Not Prepare Russell For His Next Experience
Part 9 - Russell And Grace Found That Special Honeymoon Suite
Part 10 - Beauty All Around But Russell Looking For Southbound Plane
Part 11 - Alaska Could Not Match Up With Rhine, Ga., The Goatman And Georgia Iced Tea
Part 12 - Justice Boney, Totem Poles And Old Cannery Made Alaska Interesting
Part 13 - Ferry Takes Us To The "Inside Passage"
Part 14 - Alaska's Cap'n "Hell Roaring Mike" Healy Came From Georgia
Part 15 - Skagway Greeted Us With Friendly Faces, Old Tales And Cheap Goods
Part 16 - Skagway's Badman "Soapy Smith" Was From Georgia
Part 17 - Old Skagway Reminded Us Of Old Darien, Ga.
Part 18 - Skagway Train Rode Like Georgia's Old "Nancy Hanks"
Part 19 - Gold Fields Were Unforgiving But Yukon Is Breathtaking
Part 20 - Earthquake, Sea Otters And A July "Merry Christmas"
Part 21 - Sea Otters Were Slaughtered To Brink Of Extinction But Now Protected
Part 22 - Puffins, Seals And Whales Put On Quite A Show
Part 23 - Wooly Mammoths And Wolverines Looked Ready For War
Part 24 - Muskox Visit And "Steamboat Fever" Made A Big Day
Part 25 - Tiny Motel Room, Big Smart Dog And Russell Made A Crowd

Part 26 - Steamboats Hold Some Strange Tales
Part 27 - Mounties Tried To Protect Crazy Gold Seekers
Part 28 - Steamboats, Dredges And Ferries Kept Excitement High
Part 29 - Exploding Steamboats Sing A Requiem Of Death
Part 30 - Unfortunately We Will Always Remember Chicken, Alaska
Part 31 - Sometimes The Absence Dominates The Presence
Part 32 - The Great Moose Dropping Festival – And We Missed It
Part 33 - Moose Droppings, Bingo And A Bearded Man
Part 34 - Big Steamboat, Iditarod Trainers And Our Visit To Chena Village
Part 35 - Fairbanks Was Great But Russell Was 4,439 Miles From Douglas, Georgia
Part 36 - North Pole And Santa And Wife Posed With Us For A Picture
Part 37 - Alaska's Boney Courthouse Connected To Telfair County, Ga.
Part 38 - Chief Justice Boney Was Close To China Hill, Near Jacksonville, Ga.
Part 39 - Chief Justice Boney's History Welded With His Humanity
Part 40 - Harvard Law School Was Not Ready For George Boney
Part 41 - Boney Clan, Fish Fry And Coach Bowden At The Football Reunion
Part 42 - Life Of Chief Justice Boney A Rich Legacy Of Brilliance, Common Sense And Love
Part 43 - An "Old Geezer" Alaskan Taught Engineers How To Build A Road
Part 44 - Monstrous Mosquitoes And Lawn Mowers On The Roofs
Part 45 - Picnic, Hot Springs And Walls Of Old Car Tags From Everywhere
Part 46 - Bigfoot And Canada's Sasquatch And A Similar Booger At Jacksonville, Ga.
Part 47 - Big Hay Fields, John Deere, Chuckwagons And Rolling Stores
Part 48 - Big Canada Mall, An Old Stove And A Sweet Memory Of Grandmama's Stewed Tomatoes
Part 49 - Canada's Mounties Train And Strive To Be The Best
Part 50 - Giant Paul Bunyan, "Dead-Ringers" And Some Pretty Big Men At Jacksonville, Ga.
Part 51 - We Bid Farewell – Alaska And Canada – Our Fine Memories Are Overflowing

FOREWORD

First, I believe a book should be brief – like the sermon described by a pastor. The pastor told of another pastor who arrived at a church and was ready with his points for the sermon. He also had a gavel and prepared to strike the gavel on the pulpit after each point (for emphasis). After about 15 points into the sermon the enthusiastic pastor in his fervent delivery vigorously swung the gavel and the gavel got loose from his hand and struck a lady in the second row. She was hit right on the head squarely — unconscious. After some time the lady recovered, looked around to check the situation and said, "Somebody hit me again, I can still hear him!" I will be brief. I do not desire to give you more information and/or stories that will exceed your comfort and patience. I want you to enjoy the book.

Second, I will probably send or mail the book to some of you — friends, acquaintances, history lovers and even some I do not know. You may read it, trash it or send it to others. If you like it and/or want to help the Old Jacksonville History project just send the project a donation. I will include all the details in your letter (and the book). If you do not like the book that is okay too. But do not send it back to me; keep it. Or give it to another. We don't want it returned. We are trying our best to get rid of these books!

Old Jacksonville, Ga., made me want to see Alaska. Old Jacksonville is my old hometown and the rich history even includes Alaska. In fact, several personalities came to Alaska from Georgia during the 1800s and 1900s. If you don't know where the little town of Jacksonville, Ga., just look at a good map where the Ocmulgee River does its "Big Bend." After this the Ocmulgee joins the Altamaha River and on to the Atlantic Ocean. Jacksonville is on Highway 441. Going south you go to Florida; going north you will go to North Carolina. But for the best history around you can just stay at Old Jacksonville, Georgia. The chronicles reveal some of the richest history of the state (and in cases, the nation). To accommodate your visit we have erected several history signs (next to the highway) full of interesting text and images.

As we leave Georgia and head for Alaska we invite you to go with us as we see, hear, smell and feel a new country and an exciting land.

We also travel in other states as we head for Alaska. To experience each area will add another rich niche in your memory vault. You will share with us our good days, our bad days, the grinning and the laughter. You will share all the ups and downs of this trip. You will probably decide whether you want to make the pilgrimage or stay at home! Enjoy the book. As you read you will see why Old Jacksonville, Ga., made me want to see Alaska.

And we could not have successfully completed our trip without our fellow travelers. Here is a list of our fellow travelers. Folks, thanks for your fellowship and making our Alaska trip a memorable one. We dedicate this effort to you.

(As Listed On The Geri-Gadder Alaska Adventure Tour Roster):
Juanita Morgan
Alice McDuffie
Dan & Joann Minix
Emmie Glenn
Delora Hall
Merrill & Shirley Palmer
Pecolia Ann Hughes
Kitty Coleman
John & Barbara Milhous
Julian & Joanne Williams
Doris Marchant
Russell & Grace Collins
J.L. & Doris Sutton
Bob & Pat Moos
Ruth Grinstead
Erwin & Elizabeth Wilson
Betty Tillman
Vi Taylor
Dwight & Conchita Hutchison
Hawey & Trudy Carmichael
Melva Stevens
George & Joan McPherson
Evelyn Goodroe
Bob & Pat Monroe
Al & Mary Jo Rogers
Madeline Alred
Margie Whiddon

William & Ruth Labhart
Haskell White, Tour Director/Host
Glenda White, Tour Administrator/Hostess
Kenny Gordon, Motor Coach Operator
Race Gordon, Luggage Manager

So! Here we go!

Part 1
Crying Time And Leaving Georgia For Icebergs

Alaska! Old Jacksonville, Ga., made me want to see Alaska. Right now I want to at least start our journey toward Alaska, The Great Land. It is a big country. In fact, if we superimpose the map on the former 48 United States we see that Alaska is about the fifth of that area (20%) (in size) of those four dozen "lower" states. To Alaska they live in the North; all of us in the "lower states" live in the South. That is certainly a new perspective.

And if you don't believe that is a big country just park yourself on a tour bus for 31 days and after that vehicle has rolled 10,725 miles I believe you will agree with me and Joanne, Russell and Grace Collins and all those other 42 travelers that there is consensus about the size of Alaska — big!

Also, if you forget, as I do sometimes, about those numerical numbers (as in "numb") just check your gluteus maximus for wear and tear. In fact, if you are looking for it you will find it about halfway from the back of your head and your hamstring (near back of the heel). In that rear midsection you will find etched, hopefully not permanently, the print of the texture of the bus seat. The image on my flesh looks like an embossed and depressed image, applied alternately. The work would stir any artist — the medium, the effect and especially the symmetry.

Also, Russell Collins never lets me forget that the whole idea of going to Alaska was not the brightest idea I had ever conceived. But I stick to my resolve — that it was a great adventure. Unfortunately, I am not sure my wife, Joanne, would swear to any affidavits to the above. The first night at Bainbridge, Ga., the departure place, Joanne cried, in the darkness of the motel — "I do not want to go — I want to go home." I suspected the long haul was going to be very very long — and painful. To be sure I hid the key to the Ford F-150 and hoped for better times. Times got better.

But, Joanne probably caught the venture, if not adventure, as soon as she was surrounded by icebergs and frolicked with the huge killer whales and watched awestruck the colossal collapsing of a glacier. She was all over the boat while Russell sought warmth in the enclosed place of Lu Lu Belle, the great boat. Russell was freezing. I was about halfway. But all that will have to wait. We are getting ahead.

One thing that made me want to go to Alaska actually resided in some of the places we would encounter during the trip. The first night we were in Paducah, Kentucky.

I was glad to be in Kentucky Commonwealth, home of the great General John C. Breckinridge. Breckinridge had been the United States Vice-President before he joined the Confederacy and became a general and later the Secretary of War. At the end of the Civil War he hid at Jacksonville, Ga. When the coast was clear he was given a boat near Jacksonville, Ga., at the Ocmulgee River. I am glad he got away. Later he was able to go back to Kentucky. So another reason I wanted to travel this way. Also, Kentucky has some humor and wisdom. One of the best wits was Irvin Shrewsburg Cobb who said:

"Here in Paducah one encounters, I claim, an agreeable blend of Western kindliness, and Northern enterprises, superimposed upon a Southern background. Here, I claim, more chickens are fried, more hot biscuits are eaten, more corn pone is consumed, and more genuine hospitality is offered than in any town of like size in the commonwealth."

Unfortunately, not all of Cobb's items made it to Canada (on the way to Alaska). It was not that the food was all bad, it was just different. And we were longing for good fried chicken, delicious Southern iced tea and big warm fittin' biscuits. Alas, we would not see the doings of such until we expired our trip in 31 days and set ourselves down to the Farmers Market Restaurant at Thomasville, Ga. I just about hurt myself eating at that fine place.

So, we will now take a break until we continue with another article about our trip — aiming the old bus to other points heading toward Alaska.

Credit: Geri-Gadder Tours of Bainbridge, Ga.; our fellow travelers; Paducah, KY, info; personal experiences; personal info; other sources.

Part 2
We Needed General Breckinridge And Jesse James In Our Bus Restroom

We look backward as we see the old ghost of General John C. Breckinridge of the old Kentucky Commonwealth. I am glad he was in the boat on the Ocmulgee River near Jacksonville, Ga., in May of 1865, and not in the tour bus with Russell Collins in June of 2008. General Breckinridge had enough challenge to evade the Yankees and slip out of the country when the Civil War ended. I don't know if Breckinridge could have coped with Russell Collins our friend from Douglas, Ga., on our Alaska trip. I know that it would not have worked at all if Russell had been in the Ocmulgee River boat with Breckinridge. The General probably would have desired to wind up in Alaska to evade Russell! So the time warp would have been fortunate for The General but it was not so lucky for the bus travelers. We had Russell.

But, regardless of what Russell told you, we were having a good time as the old bus moved northward toward St. Joseph, Missouri, our second night of our journey. This was a special place for me because that was where Jesse James was killed by the old coward Bob Ford. After all, Jesse Woodson James was related to many of our Old Jacksonville, Ga., folks because the Woodson-Willcox connection goes directly to three sons, the Willcoxes (Wilcoxes) of Old Jacksonville, Ga., Dolley Madison, former lady of President James Madison and Jesse Woodson James, infamous outlaw.

Along with Jesse James we even talked about sports as the old bus rambled on. The day's big item was the Georgia Bulldogs - the football team — being noticed as No. 1 in national ratings. Someone raised his index finger and said, "No.1!" It's good to be No.1. Russell frowned because he does not like sports.

In this elation of a winning team No.1 rating, and enjoying the countryside as it changed from Kentucky to Missouri, and thinking of Jesse James, I realized that the regular restroom break would be quite awhile up the road. Doing a little calculation with the time expired from the last break, speed of the bus, the remaining mileage to the next regular stop, the initial time of swallowing my water pill, and a fast anxiety check, I knew it would be necessary (quickly) — to engage Plan B. Plan B is designated as Back — as, at the little emergency restroom at the BACK OF THE BUS.

This mysterious appliance in the rear bus must be noted because it is probably the most important fixture in that tour bus. Many sweating, anxious, painful and even praying people have sought that little secluded enclosed capsule as a last resort. It has saved innumerable persons and without it there would have been physical, emotional and mental disasters for those identified users.

It is a special place — almost indescribable — in other words, you are not to use it but on the other hand, if you just have to use it, go ahead. It was like a relative taboo that was not a taboo because it was relative. A reluctant resort.

But even that sublime paradox does not always work with the secret smooth operation desired by the user. For example, the bus driver forgets to leave the light "ON" in the little restroom. Pitch dark. That little relay switch is on the dashboard at the FRONT, just next to the driver, Kenny Gordon. The tour director, Rev. Haskell White, is there with the driver (up there FRONT when I have to go to the BACK!).

Now, between me and Kenny and Haskell, are 45 satisfied persons, pleasantly viewing scenes, sleeping or daydreaming. Some are reading. Some are just sitting. I would not disturb these people for anything. In addition, Haskell does not like for you to shout manual unannounced assorted news all over the bus. Ask for the mike.

Waving, I was lucky — I caught Haskell's eye and attention and held up my index finger. Haskell smiled the best smile I had ever seen. Evidently, he thought I had called winning No. 1 Bulldogs again. But I was calling another No.1 — back restroom! Haskell didn't know. He continued that smile — like his face was frozen. He held it. I envied his confidence. And his smile.

About then, unexpectedly, careening forward — abruptly and awkwardly — due to some slower vehicle (or animal) getting in front of our bus, I grabbed a few seats as I was catapulted up/down the aisle in the wrong direction. Righting my legs and arms I made a quick retreat back to the restroom, grabbed the handle of the restroom and commenced to holler. With this, my floating teeth told me that No.1 was imminent. And it wasn't football.

"Haskelllll, turn ON the light!" It was time to speak up.

I will continue next time. Alaska is going to be a long interesting road. Hang on!

Credit: Geri-Gadder Tours of Bainbridge, Ga.; our fellow travelers; KY and MO info; personal experiences; personal info; other sources.

HERE WE ARE IN ST. LOUIS, MO -- AT "THE ARCH"

Russell said, "Julian, where are they (Grace and Joanne - the wives)?

Julian said, "They might have left and gone back to Georgia."

Russell said, "They better not leave me up here."

Julian said, "Here they come! They said they were looking in shops."

TRANSLATION: THEY SHOPPED

Russell Collins

Can't Wait For ALASKA!

JESSE JAMES, AGE 34, HOME OF ST. JOSEPH, MISSOURI, WHEN HE WAS MURDERED BY BOB FORD IN 1882.

OLDTIMERS OF OLD JACKSONVILLE, GA., SAY THAT JESSE WOODSON JAMES VISITED THE AREA AND SWAM IN WILLCOX LAKE IN THE COLD CLEAR WATER. JESSE JAMES IS ALSO KIN TO THE WILLCOX (WILCOX) FAMILY. SOME OF THESE ARE STILL AROUND OLD JACKSONVILLE, GA.

DEVOTED HUSBAND AND FATHER JESSE WOODSON JAMES SEPT. 5, 1847 MURDERED APR. 3, 1882 BY A TRAITOR AND COWARD WHOSE NAME IS NOT WORTHY TO APPEAR HERE

IT IS SAID THAT ONE MARK WILCOX RODE WITH JESSE JAMES IN MISSOURI.

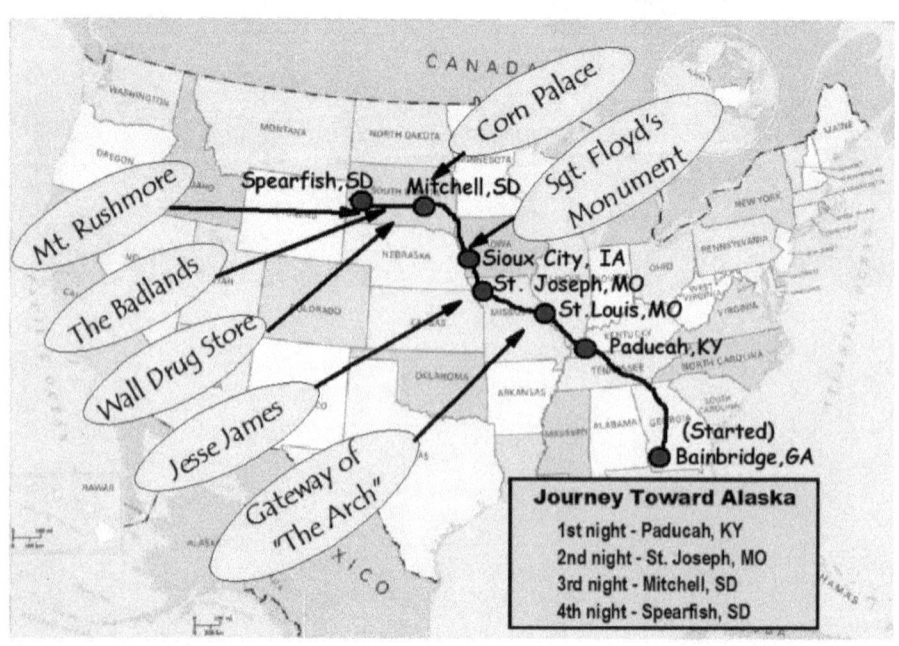

Journey Toward Alaska
1st night - Paducah, KY
2nd night - St. Joseph, MO
3rd night - Mitchell, SD
4th night - Spearfish, SD

Part 3
Restroom Extrication, Breckinridge's Relatives And The Corn Palace

Before I continue the trip I need to extricate myself from this little emergency restroom in the back of the bus. I am still in here. When I left you I had just gotten into the restroom as the light finally turned on. With this new dimension (the light) I could look around in that little restroom. I looked around in there. There were printed instructions on the stainless steel wall indicating that I was not to stand up in there. Just sit down. There was an emphasis: Only sit down on the receptacle. However, I decided real quick that I did not like those instructions. If I was going to be slinged-shot from my tiny cubicle I was going to be vertical (standing up), crouched right and alertly and braced (good).

It was good that I was braced. After only about two minutes after I took this stance I felt another jarring jolt which coincided with a tremendous noise from the bus. It had struck a bad hole in the road and I just about came out of that little restroom. And it was a chore to keep from flying out of there. After settling down I had to figure which way I was headed. After a little confusion on this I pressed the little button that spews blue liquid around in the commode and flushes the bowl. After that I squirted the provided anti-bacterial waterless hand sanitizer onto my hands and I was ready. You had to use this because there is not a little neat lavoratory out there in that little restroom. After getting squared away and checking to see if I was presentable I started out. At least, I thought. The latch froze up. Or at least I thought it malfunctioned. Actually I was malfunctioning. But after all that I could understand. I had turned it the wrong direction. With another try — the little door opened.

And I was again out into civilization. Fresh air again — comparably. Our interested fellow travelers were there (those awake); some curious were looking at me to see if I had survived. Others were trying to be polite by keeping their faces in their books and newspapers and brochures. But, there was our old bus — still running. It had taken us many miles and it was going to make it many many more miles. If I could just imagine!

The next stop would be Sioux City, Iowa. There was an imposing monument of some 100 feet high. It was the monument of Sgt. Charles Floyd, only man to die in the Lewis-Clark Expedition. He was a brother of Gov. Floyd of Virginia. The family had a Breckinridge in it. That made me feel good because I felt like these folks were relatives of General Breckinridge who hid out at Old Jacksonville, Ga. In fact, I know they were relatives because I looked up the family lineage. Same folks.

However, this warm relationship of old General Breckinridge-Old Jacksonville, Ga., hiding in 1865 and the fact that Sgt. Floyd was a connection did not matter a whit with my wife, Joanne. If she saw the monument it was out of the bus window. I got Russell and Grace to pose by the monument. But Joanne is very selective about these sights. Also if she is in a good book it takes a compelling sight to interrupt her reading. Joanne just commented that it looked a lot like Washington's Monument. Now I knew — she did look!

It wasn't a little while before we were reaching a little town named Mitchell, South Dakota. But it is famous — for its corn! These folks did not just plant corn, cook corn and eat corn! They had a palace of corn! It was named The Corn Palace. We never saw the likes of that place. No, if there was any place that just took a place with absolutely nothing and made it something then this was the place! It is tremendous what a cooperative community can do if it puts its wheel to the grindstone. Now all of America goes to see The Corn Palace. Exquisite drawings, murals, creative works, etc., "you-name-it" is made of corn — just corn! And the whole community is into this corn. They even play their basketball games in The Corn Palace. And they change the whole theme of The Corn Palace each year! Amazing! Corniest place I ever saw!

Well, we are now down the road near Murdo, South Dakota, and the Old 1880 Town is just ahead. Take a look at the picture — doesn't Cisco the horse look real? And we will continue in another article.

Credit: Geri-Gadder Tours of Bainbridge, Ga.; our fellow travelers; KY,IA,MO,SD info; personal experiences; personal info; other sources

Russell and Grace

Are getting ready for Alaska! Russell is already smiling!

This is Sgt. Floyd's Monument at Sioux City, Iowa.

Sgt. Floyd was only person to die during Lewis-Clark Expedition

Part 4
Stuffed Horses, Old Schoolhouses And The Badlands

I certainly enjoyed the sights of Old 1880 Original Town at Murdo, South Dakota, and would rate it with a "very good." Of course, I am not all that good about judging horses and I have to agree with Russell, Grace and Joanne. Cisco ("Buck") a horse in the movie "Dances With Wolves" by Kevin Costner was probably stuffed. But he sure looked real!

The Old 1880 Original Town was interesting from its birth. Some fellow came along on the prairie and established a service station. Then someone decided to add a building and have a "western attraction." It seems that fate just fell into the pot luck. A movie company came to town and established an old town "set" to the adjoining property. In a cold winter the movie company returned home and left the "set" to the lucky man. His Old Town was now a reality and he started finding contents to go inside those buildings.

Evidently, the venture flourished and now all America can come there and enjoy the fruits of that labor. As I walked around I looked in most of the 30 odd buildings and other attractions. I especially reminisced when I got to the old school with the big bell. We used to have one like that at Workmore School. It was fun to pull the rope and hear that bell. I could not resist but a little boy with his family appeared and started pulling the rope and the bell sounded off! I was glad that he could take my place because I believe I enjoyed seeing his eyes brightened as he really enjoyed ringing that bell! Made my day.

I also looked with memories as I looked at the old desks with the inkwell hole. We used to corral the girls' hair and work their long hair into that inkwell. Sometimes we would take our pencil and place it underneath the inkwell and tie it with a rubber band — with their hair! The girls seemed to enjoy the attention. Sometimes it was not too funny if the teacher caught us doing this! We had a lot of tricks at Workmore School but the teachers were usually equal to those mischievous concoctions.

Of course, Russell was right there at the Wells-Fargo Stagecoach and I tried to depict Russell on that stage — as the driver. I think Russell would fit right into that position and would know just how to handle that situation. He reads enough of those Western paperbacks to be an expert about all that. In fact, if Russell had not given up the driver's seat when he did we would have missed our bus.

We were not that far away from Deadwood and when I saw Wyatt Earp's 44 Smith & Wesson I thought about his being in Deadwood for a short period in 1876. General Custer had caused a lot of stir when he announced "gold is in them thar hills." Folks came by the hordes and that is when the Indians were not welcome to visit their own homes and sacred places. I think Russell would have bought Earp's pistol if he could have managed it.

I especially liked the old doctor's office in the second story of The Emporium. We had better be glad we live in this technologically advanced age. The instruments and the results were pretty documented in a very graphic way! No way do I want to go back to the old days!

But time was up and we had to go. I could have stayed hours more at the Old Town but we cranked the old bus and headed for The Badlands.

The Badlands is an area you would just have to see. I don't see how human beings, or any animal, could survive there. It is a desolate, barren and unforgiving place. I would not even want to do much but pass through that domain.

I took a shot of our good friends J.L. and Doris Sutton of Dahlonega, Georgia. You can see from the picture that The Badlands is appropriately named. I bet they have enough scorpions and rattlesnakes to furnish a few trainloads.

I also want to thank J.L. and Doris for helping us keep Russell straight. At times I wondered if we would get through the trip without losing Russell. But about the time I thought he might leave us a great wonder of nature would appear and Russell would be reinvigorated. I think J.L. even had Russell looking for a grizzly bear and a Dall sheep. Even for Russell there are hopes of wonders! North to Alaska!

Credit: Geri-Gadder Tours of Bainbridge, Ga.; our fellow travelers; KY,IA,MO,SD info; personal experiences; personal info; other sources.

We Enjoyed Alaska – But Russell Just About Killed Us!

Russell here reliving the Wild West times of the good old days!

OLD DOCTOR'S OFFICE UPSTAIRS
OLD FIRE ENGINE
WYATT EARP'S 44 SMITH & WESSON
OLD 1880 TOWN - MURDO, SOUTH DAKOTA

Part 5
Old Jacksonville, Ga.,
And Murdo, South Dakota, Had Connections

Here we were — Murdo, South Dakota. Just out of the box I would say there is absolutely no connection with Jacksonville, Georgia, and Murdo, South Dakota. I mean there are accidents, coincidental happenings and amazing rabbit pullings going on everywhere but there is no way anyone or anything from that south Georgia of Jacksonville ever had a "hey, partner" to do with that stretched out place called Murdo, South Dakota, and surroundings. Absolutely. Nothing.

But you always get a surprise if you are traveling. Here we are: Murdo, South Dakota. Great expanses of land and land and land. Now we were looking at all those antiques and the wonders of the 1800's we talked about in the last article. The Old Town of 1880's — Murdo, South Dakota. It was fun.

But in the back of my head I knew something was vaguely familiar about these surroundings. I hadn't been there because I had never been close to South Dakota. But my friend, Jim Bland, solved my pondering. He reminded me that I was very near right in the middle of his hunting patch!

Jim Bland, a friend of mine, was someone I saw more in our younger ages when we lived at Jacksonville, Ga., and later, both lived at Douglas, Ga. In between he was lucky to marry Gail Ricketson of Broxton and that made his worth go way up! He worked with the Mack dealership in Douglas and wound up in Winston Salem, North Carolina. I think it would be an understatement to say that he has been successful. In fact, I think he owns four truck dealerships in the area. I knew he would be successful in "many moons back" when he borrowed our Jacksonville shop to rebuild his 1956 Chevy. Right out of the box he cleaned the place up, laid a clean white sheet on the work table, lined his tools on this sheeted table and commenced to finesse those tools with the various parts of that automobile. Looking at all that I thought I was looking at a doctor operating. Smooth. I decided he would do okay.

Back to his current home of North Carolina. So, with all that work Jim likes to get away from time to time and goes to nearby Murdo, South Dakota — just where we were. Why there? It is probably one of the best places in the world for hunting pheasants. And Jim can enjoy the outdoors and treat his customers for some mighty good pheasant hunting.

Jim started telling me about those pheasants. Made me want to hunt pheasants and I don't even hunt. You have to do a little bit different from hunting turkeys. That pheasant that flushes out in the vast acreage is a beauty of a bird to see. It seems the best veterans of the field can freeze — petrified with a dry mouth and a missed shot when one of those majestic fowls takes flight. You can just get overwhelmed!

And to digress just a moment — about acreage. What acreage around South Dakota! Jim Bland tells me about a good friend of his in South Dakota named Jim Nachtigal. Mr. Nachtigal is a young man of 83 years of age and loves folks to drop in. Because Mr. Nachtigal, of German descent, and his wife Mary, do not have people coming around frequently. Not that Mr. Nachtigal is not a fine fellow and does not like socializing. That is not the problem. The problem is this: he owns approximately 30,000 acres at his farm. The couple with five children might go for days, weeks or months without seeing anyone. But they have a lot of work to do. But they do like to see Jim Bland. And Jim Bland likes to see the Nachtigals. They hunt and they socialize and it is a good time.

On the next day they take to the big field - about five "drivers" are spaced along about 80 rows of corn or sunflower or whatever and start "driving" the pheasants; a few on the flanks called "wingers" look for the pheasants trying to flush that way; the "blockers" are stationed at the end of the field. As this pincer operation proceeds the pheasant can run or flush. The good hunter gets one. If not, the pheasant sees another day without visiting the eating table.

I've about made up my mind that you can see about anything at or near Murdo, South Dakota. Even the famous "General Lee" is there at the car Pioneer Museum. The "01" Dodge Charger of "Dukes of Hazzard" was good. But it couldn't beat that 1956 dynamo souped-up V-8 black Chevy that Jim Bland built in our shop at Jacksonville,

Georgia. He was that good.

Credit: Geri-Gadder Tours of Bainbridge, Ga.; our fellow travelers; KY,IA,MO,SD info; Jim Bland info; personal experiences; personal info; other sources.

Old Town - 1880 - Murdo, South Dakota

Jim Bland of North Carolina, Formerly of Jacksonville, GA

Hunting South Dakota Pheasants

Part 6
Found Free Ice Water
Before Seeing Mount Rushmore

I just knew that Russell would love this next site (and sight!) — The Wall Drug Store at Wall, South Dakota. In fact, it is about the only thing out here that is free! For miles we could see the signs — "Stop at Wall Drug — Free Ice Water." And various slogans and sayings. After hearing all about Wall Drug and the free ice water you began to get thirsty and want to stop there. So we stopped. I have never seen such a crowded-up bunch in one little place in the world!

They say a good average number of folks coming in at the drug store hovers around 20,000 each day. Several millions of curious tourists come to Wall Drug Store each year. You see so much stuff there you are actually dumbfounded and a little numb by the "exhibits" there. I will not try to explain all those — some smooth and rough — venues, some serious and some quite comical. You will just have to come to see and do your own "appreciation" of all that showmanship.

I can tell you one thing though! Wall Drug Store has the best roast beef and mashed potatoes with gravy! And you get all you need as you eat there with another 530 folks. That is the number you can seat at capacity and it seems to be about filled at all times when we were there.

Sometime if you are smart, and are lucky, you can do some spectacular things. The little drug store started in 1931 was not doing much. But Dorothy Hustead, the wife of Ted Hustead (owner), suggested that they just go out on the highways and place signs — "Free Ice Water." The line was forming before they got back there. And the lines are still coming. Certainly a stroke of creativity.

After we got our free ice water, our very reasonable lunch, some bought knickknacks and some got the 5 cents cup of coffee, we departed for Mount Rushmore.

You want to see Mt. Rushmore, also in South Dakota, but getting close to the borders of Wyoming and Montana. I noticed one thing about this great stone monument of the four presidents — George

Washington, Thomas Jefferson, Theodore Roosevelt, Abraham Lincoln. It does not matter how many pictures you take or get from the postcards. The views, someway, sometimes subtly, and sometimes pronounced, seem to be different. Sometime it is the angle, sometime the sky, sometime the color. Or something else. It always seems different.

I think it best to convey the feelings of the sculptor, Gutzon Borglum:

Mount Rushmore National Memorial (Shrine of Democracy)

"A monument's dimensions should be determined by the importance to civilization of the events commemorated. We are not here trying to carve an epic, portray a moonlight scene, or write a sonnet; neither are we dealing with mystery or tragedy, but rather the constructive and dramatic moments or crises in our amazing history." Gutzon Borglum

And Gutzon Borglum was the same man who worked on The Confederate Memorial at Stone Mountain, Georgia. Dying in 1941, his son Lincoln Borglum finished the work at Mt. Rushmore.

The American Natives also got involved with Mt. Rushmore because they contend it belongs to them. They say a treaty was broken. To add to this note, the Indians are now working on their own monument called "Crazy Horse." When finished the monument will be a colossal figure — about 563 feet high and wider than this. That would be something to see. That undertaking is taking place about 17 miles from Mount Rushmore.

Well, I had better try to round up my fellow travelers — Russell and Grace Collins and Joanne Williams. It is difficult to get them still so we can get a picture group. I think they are so excited by this trip they just cannot stay still for a moment.

Credit: Geri-Gadder Tours of Bainbridge, Ga.; our fellow travelers; KY, IA, MO, SD info; personal experiences; personal info; other sources.

Part 7
Sundance Kid And General Custer Met Us Down The Road

Although we were not allowed to spend much time with the old outlaws of the legends of the area we would be remiss if we did not at least give a nod toward that epic era. Notwithstanding the fact these outlaws were outside the legal "deadline" definitions (physical and lawful), those unsavory and stealing personalities were parts of what went on in the Old West.

As we leave Spearfish, South Dakota, and head for nearby environs — a little bit of northeastern Sundance, Wyoming, we could not help but think of the notorious gang called the Hole In The Wall Gang (The Wild Bunch) that was led by two men called Sundance Kid and Butch Cassidy. Harry Longabaugh was caught in his early tenure and placed in the jail at Sundance, Wyoming. Evidently he liked the name of the town and after eighteen months (jail) he took the name "Sundance" as his nickname.

From the picture of The Gang it seems that the members had quite fashionable clothes and this natty attire is seen in this photograph (this article). In fact, we decided this photo had exhibited the best-of-the-side of the gangsters. Following this, and reflecting on the various styles of Western characters, we felt that Russell Collins (allowing an anachronism) would love to be in this 1890's particular photo. We have tried to insert Russell in this photo (center back) and it seems that Russell fits right in there with the others. We especially like his hat. His hands are maybe a little bit too big but if he had rustled steers, caught moving trains and carried big side arms, then maybe his hands would have been that big in the 1890s.

But, we cannot tarry with The Hole In The Wall Gang as we are leaving Wyoming toward Custer's Last Stand — the Little Bighorn Battlefield — in Montana. As our big bus negotiate a few turns off the bigger roads we slowly approach that killing field.

As we approach the Little Bighorn entrance the large sign seems to have a soldier present - an eerie apparition — the ghost of Brevet Major General (Lt. Col.) George A. Custer. Sitting right there. Those American soldiers and horses and many Indians perished that day in June of 1876. But the presence is still there and will probably always be there. There is a presence.

As we trudge along those bleak hills interspersed by distant plains we can internalize that desperate moment — "Custer's Last Stand." The little wind stirring is not enough to get rid of the poignant ill-fated frame that we are now enclosed. We feel and hear the loud silence of the defeat of brave warriors of the 7th U.S. Cavalry.

But there were other brave warriors on the other side — the American Natives. They were desperately trying to hold on to hope — of surviving and maintaining a culture and a civilization. Most had already been placed on reservations. But a sizable portion had sneaked back in and returned to fight.

Many tales are told of that fight in the Little Bighorn but probably a lot of truth is lost. Some said that Custer's ego got him in trouble and got him and all his men killed. Some said he would not take along the big Gatling guns because those guns would hold him back and would slow him down. Some said other outfits were offered to Custer but he said, "the 7th can handle everything." Another person said that Custer could be admired. Another person would say just the opposite.

But looking around the graves and markers and the memorial plaques and other signs one gets the idea that the battlefield is not "Custer's Battlefield" but it is the "Little Bighorn Battlefield" because American Natives (Indians) are determined to get some exposure relative to their role in the battle.

And you can see some graves and/or markers there. And some of those soldiers came from the 7th Cavalry. And some horses. And some Indians. But the body of Custer is not enshrined in this token marker. His remains were taken to West Point. I suppose someone made sure he joined his classmates at the academy by the Hudson River. But his presence is at the Little Bighorn.

Credit: Geri-Gadder Tours of Bainbridge, Ga.; our fellow travelers; KY, IA, MO, SD, WY, MT info; personal experiences; personal info; other sources.

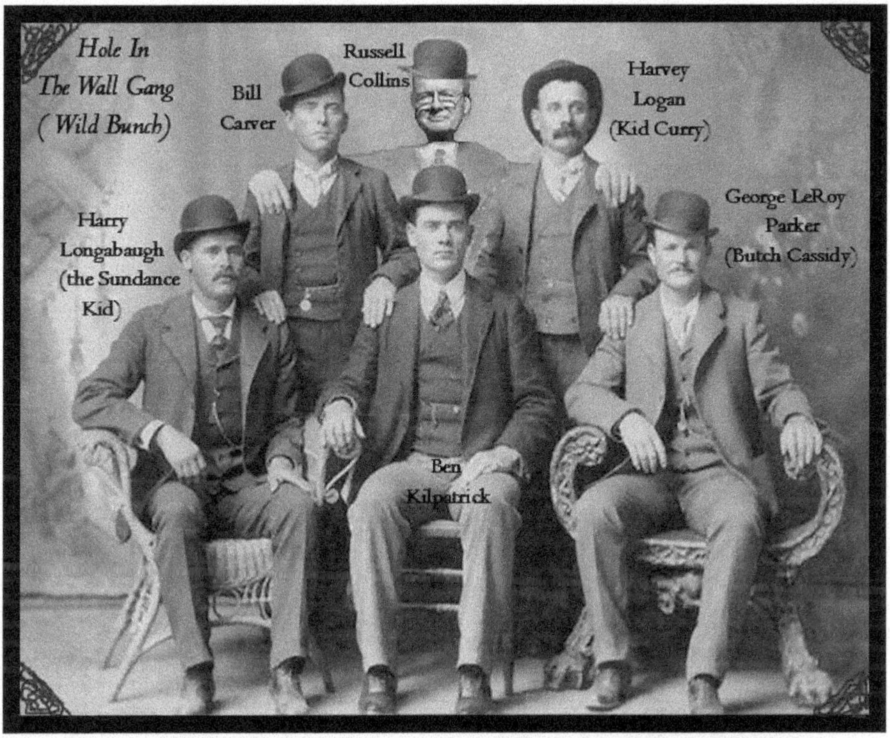

Survivors of Battle of the Little Big Horn (1876)
At Reunion in Black Hills, SD, Sept. 2, 1948

Little Warrior | Pemmican | Little Soldier | Dewey Beard | John Sitting Bull | High Eagle | Iron Hawk | Comes Again

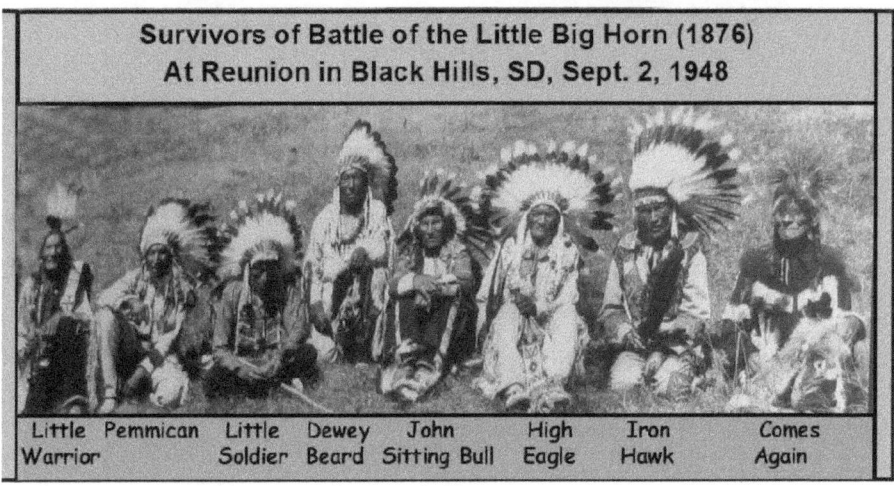

Part 8
Little Bighorn Did Not Prepare Russell For His Next Experience

We leave this Little Bighorn Battlefield and include the ghostly image of Custer as he sits on one of the pillars on the entrance sign. Looking at this image I cannot think but remember that Custer was associated with great General Phil Kearny in the Civil War. Kearny was later killed by Sgt. John McCrimmon of Jacksonville, Ga., when the sharpshooting Southern soldier dropped Kearny in the rain and mud of Ox Hill at Chantilly, Virginia.

Earlier, Kearny chose Custer as his first aide-de-camp on his staff because the daring courageous Kearny saw those same charging and reckless characteristics and devil-may-care abandonment in younger Custer. And Custer did not disappoint Kearny at all. Throughout the Civil War Custer was in the thick of battle and gained much recognition. In fact, he was so successful he was made a major-general in his early twenties. As strange as it is, General Kearny and Custer met death in quite unlikely and unusual situations/places.

As we leave the Little Bighorn Battlefield we leave with many emotions about what happened in those terrible two days of June in 1876. But the Civil War had ended, gold was discovered in the Black Hills and the hordes of people came to change the way of the American Natives (Indians) — a way that had endured for a long time. War was inevitable.

As we left the scene and some of those thoughts we transferred our attentions to Russell Collins because he was already complaining about the long bus ride. And to tell the truth he had some substance for argument. The posterior position for the anatomy can just stand so much in a day's time.

We will just pause to let you know how many miles we have now covered on the road. By Day 1 we had already traveled 628 miles by Kentucky. The second day at St. Joseph, MO, had tacked on another 523 miles. By the time we reached Mitchell, South Dakota, we had registered another 343 miles. By the time we reached Mt. Rushmore we had added another 315 miles. And now we are leaving Little Bighorn and by the time we reach the Yogo Inn at Lewistown, Montana, we were marking up another 324 miles. Russell was getting antsy.

But the long ride was cushioned and made enjoyable by the fantastic scenery coming up into our views as we looked almost unbelievably on these beautiful panoramas.

But what we had forgotten was something looming ahead — the Canadian Customs located on the border. Our bus, and all of us, had to "pass muster" to get from the United States to Canada. We also had to present our passports. Maybe, no problem.

But seeing those serious looking border guards/Canadian Mounties/policemen or whatever they were called did not make us feel exactly comfortable.

And then something happened.

A stern agent with dark uniform called loudly, "Russell Collins. Leave your position and come out of the bus!"

I thought, *Great day*. They have smelled that forbidden fresh fruit — a no-no for passengers going over a border. Poor Russell had cherished and cuddled and cared for that big juicy apple and that border lawman was about to get that apple. But this "apple" was not in the suitcase. The "apple" was stuck in Russell's Adam's apple because he was not enjoying the direction this was taking.

"Mr. Collins. I am looking at your passport and some of the information on our computers. We need to ask you some questions."

What the Canadian lawmen asked Russell was not about hoarding the apple. This was way past that and Russell was very concerned about the questions.

"Mr. Collins! Have you ever been in prison?"

This interrogation was not funny, especially to Russell — and it was causing a concern for all of us. Are they going to detain Russell? Will all of us be detained? Would they put us up in a room or what? Don't see any food around here either! This could be serious.

Luckily, the Canadians, and somebody on the bus, were getting a little laugh. But Russell can take it — at least after he swallowed his Adam's apple and ate the real apple the first chance he got!

I could already see — Russell was going to, intentionally or not, provide us a lot of reflection, reaction, information — and entertainment!

We Enjoyed Alaska – But Russell Just About Killed Us! 33

Credit: Geri-Gadder Tours of Bainbridge, Ga.; our fellow travelers; KY, IA, MO, SD, WY, MT, Canada info; personal experiences; personal info; other sources.

Part 9
Russell And Grace Found That Special Honeymoon Suite

If you weren't with us last article, our fine spokesman, color analyst and opinion expert, Russell Collins, was interrogated quite pointedly and seriously by the Canadian border lawmen; and we thought they were going to keep Russell. But, we were glad to get out of that Canadian border check — with Russell with us — freed and intact.

For the rest of the trip our apples never tasted quite the same. We had always heard the Canadian Mounties "get their man." We thought they had Russell for sure. One fellow asked us if Canada kept Russell. Another said that Russell looked mighty suspicious. But regardless of how bad the cards were stacked the Canadians let Russell get back on our bus and take his seat. Usually Russell stays in the aisle talking to others but for about four hours he stayed right in his seat. Real quiet.

But, "even that too will pass" and we were forgetting Mounties and looking for the next motel. Up until now the rooms and beds were more or less nondescript. While adequate we were still looking for an interesting and different lodging suite. Russell, especially, is always looking at the rooms — right off. He heads right for the room to check it out. In a moment he was back to inform me and Joanne that he and Grace had found the gold premium as far as beds were concerned. He eagerly beckoned us to come quickly to look at this find. He had never seen a bed like this bed. I had also never seen a bed that looked like that either — it was certainly different. If you look at the picture in this article you will see why Russell was excited about the bed. It was the "special honeymoon suite" of that motel. I was a little envious of Russell's good luck on getting this privilege but I told him he might better check under the bed — and make sure two newlywed beavers were not present. They would love those bedposts!

But ahead is coming some of the most beautiful scenes — the

majestic and towering Canadian Rockies. The valleys and rivers and trees and tiers of multicolored mountains, topped by scintillating snow could not be caught by an easel or the quick motion of a camera. You just had to see to believe — and then, it was difficult to believe that the scene could be real.

And for a climax of beauty and splendor we are driving to a spot of an almost unequal setting — Lake Louise. We absorbed ourselves with this majesty because we wanted the memory to last.

The imposing giant mountain stands like a straddled and divided sky — the pristine water is close enough to touch — the glacier coming down the chute adds to the energy and the resplendent jewel of nature amidst our presence. I said right there — with God so "here" how could folks doubt the Deity? Only God could create and orchestrate this symphony — only He could do something like so magnificent. Amazing — awesome.

But, in all this the moneychangers had to be circulating. The Canadians had a great lodge there at Lake Louise and they were eager to get our U.S. money and return to us their "loonies" (one dollar coins) and their "toonies" (two dollar coins). And after we tried to exchange these currencies we were all about "looney." It would be good to be back to the great USA and hold a regular dollar. But right now we just tried to think we were getting the right change for our butter pecan ice cream. But that was sure good ice cream. And at about now Grace was going to have to readjust Russell's attitude. And we'll be back with that later.

Credit: Geri-Gadder Tours of Bainbridge, Ga.; our fellow travelers; KY, IA, MO, SD, WY, MT, Canada info; personal experiences; personal info; other sources.

Russell and Grace very pleased with this honeymoon suite - They had been looking for this decor.

Part 10
Beauty All Around But Russell Looking For Southbound Plane

We were now in Canada and the scenery was beautiful. But the more Russell thought about being headed more away from Douglas, Ga., he became anxious. Here we have gone about seven days and we have to go 31 days! A fast calculation told Russell we had about 24 days left.

This calculation also started Russell thinking. He had a faraway look in his eyes. He started talking about how he could get on the plane and be back in Douglas, Ga., real quick. If you know Russell it doesn't do for Russell to dwell very long on some possibility. If he starts massaging his brain muscles he endeavors to make that possibility into a reality.

Especially, he was very hyper as we neared Calgary, a large city, in Alberta, Canada. His graphically "explained" details began to make us think Russell was going to leave the excursion and head for home; he had a fixation about Calgary and the planes over there at the city airport. Somebody better do something about Russell.

Grace did. Somehow the feminine entity's portion of a married couple just seems to have a way of explaining — crystal clear — even when the problem is difficult and the hazy cobwebs have obscured good prudence and the spider's work has played havoc with sweet discretion.

But Grace threw down the gauntlet and Russell began to see that Grace was getting slightly irritated with his last "disappearing/leaving" strategies. Grace's ultimata included no more about talk of "deserting the ship"; no more complaining about the trip, itinerary, events, or real or imaginary problems stemming from same; no more conversation with fellow travelers which would invite disconcerting mental or physical anguish. In other words, the tickets have been paid and will not be returned; the complaining must cease; the plane will not have us on it; and furthermore, we are going to get a better attitude, and while we are here, we are going to try to enjoy it.

I think that summary made us all feel grateful that Grace had taken the time to review the travel etiquette and guidelines. Simple. Just crank up the old bus, take a seat, see the sights, and do it all again tomorrow.

But every bend is different and we are enjoying it all and appreciate the fact that God could create such nature's majesty. The Canadian Rockies stand mightily imposing and spectacular as these mighty stalwarts display unforgettable sights. Sight after sight. I never knew that these great expanses were so extensive. On and on and on. Green in the valleys. White on the snowcaps. A camera cannot realize or redeem this beauty. Impossible.

We leave you also with a picture of beautiful Peyto Lake, one of the premier favorites of tourists. Left to right on the Peyto Lake scenic overlook are Julian Williams, Joanne Williams, Grace Collins and Russell Collins.

In this Banff area these moving glaciers, the turquoise pristine waters, the lofty mountains, the wildlife roaming the range and the fresh air give testimony of something special. These memories are etched forever. And you wonder how many thousands of years have been exposed to the footprints of mankind in this place. And many of those bones still grace the ground; or at least, the dust. A lot of investment.

Credit: Geri-Gadder Tours of Bainbridge, Ga.; our fellow travelers; KY, IA, MO, SD, WY, MT, Canada info; personal experiences; personal info; other sources.

Scenic Overlook at Peyto Lake Near Lake Louise, Alberta, Canada

We thought Russell might try to get away from us in this last city - Calgary. If he did not catch this plane he would be stranded for the whole trip - but Grace threw a monkey wrench in his plan.

Peyto Lake

Part 11
Alaska Could Not Match Up With Rhine, Ga., The Goatman And Georgia Iced Tea

Well, last weekend we carried "some of Alaska" to Rhine, Ga., which is up the river road 20 miles west of Jacksonville, Ga. What we carried there were some of the Old Jacksonville, Ga., Photo Picture Plates depicting a couple of scenes about North Pole, Alaska. We included Santa Claus and Mrs. Santa Claus who were nice enough to pose with us. We will show you that one when we get to the North Pole.

But we had a wonderful time in Rhine, Ga., as those Pondtown Festival folks up there really went to great efforts to make it a very enjoyable and successful day. I believe they had the best crowd ever and more vendor spaces were occupied and that activity was stirring. We sold a lot of Old Jacksonville, Ga. Photo Picture Plates and one lady up there even bought a plate of "The Goatman." The Goatman came through Jacksonville and Rhine and almost every town and city in the State of Georgia. My father and the Goatman almost had a fight because the Goatman was whipping a baby goat; and Daddy never liked to see anybody bother with a baby — even a goat!

We were so glad to see Beal and Evelyn Halbrook from Dawson, Ga., and they came and bought the plates of the Sharon Baptist Church and the drawing of Sharon Church. Beal also purchased a picture of a fish that was only discovered recently; the actual picture was of the World Record Largemouth Bass — found in some of the stuff of some relatives who passed that on to us to enjoy. We put it on a plate. That World Record fish was caught near Jacksonville, Ga., in 1932 by George Perry.

Up at Rhine we thought about some of the towns we visited in Canada — trying to get to Alaska. Right after we rescued Russell

Collins trying to stowaway in a plane to get back to Georgia, we arrived in the little town of McBride, British Columbia, Canada.

It was a nice place but not nice as Jacksonville, Ga., and Rhine, Ga. The restaurant had good food and we were so hungry and things were going so good Russell asked the waitress if she had "a regular Georgia glass of iced tea." The waitress said, "Oh, yes, I will get you some of that!" Unfortunately, she came back later and gave us the news: "I am sorry; the kitchen manager said we could not make iced tea until tomorrow." Well, Russell, frowned because he knew if we continued with his anticipated deteriorating itinerary we would be rolling into Smithers, British Columbia, Canada, the next day as our iced tea was being prepared miles away. We wondered who got our iced tea at McBride.

Russell was right. When we arrived in Smithers and asked about the iced tea it was worse than McBride. The waitress said, "I will get you some Southern iced tea right away." She never came back with the iced tea. We sipped our water. Russell frowned again. I knew that Canada was not impressing Russell at all. About that time an airplane way up in the clouds passed by; Russell just wistfully looked up and frowned again and shook his head. He would sure like to be on that plane. And it looked like it was headed in the direction of Georgia.

But things were looking up. We were coming up next to Prince Rupert, British Columbia, Canada. With that name it would have to be something. It was something. No air conditioning and the London lady using the room just before we moved in left us a memory. She left her coffee grounds in the sink and it was stopped up — good! The nice maintenance man came and took the plumbing apart and got us going. He said, "Those London ladies do it every time." I don't believe we want to go to England. The options are getting fewer.

Credit: Geri-Gadder Tours of Bainbridge, Ga.; our fellow travelers; KY, IA, MO, SD, WY, MT, Canada info; personal experiences; personal info; other sources.

Russell saw the Bear Mountie swallow something. He thinks it was iced tea!

Moving vehicles appear small (arrows) in this Glacier (Canada) Note park vehicles in the right foreground

Part 12
Justice Boney, Totem Poles And Old Cannery Made Alaska Interesting

Going to the Pondtown Festival, as we passed by China Hill, Ga., about eight miles from Jacksonville, Ga., and about twelve miles from Rhine, Ga., I thought about the Justice George F. Boney. He was the Chief Justice of the Supreme Court of Alaska from 1969-72. He was killed in a boating accident. He is buried at China Hill at Bethel Methodist Church Cemetery. He is right out there about the middle of the cemetery. A young man — only 42 years of age.

One of the reasons I went to Alaska was to see a place loved by Justice Boney — Alaska. Specifically, I wanted to see Anchorage, the city of the justices — the supreme court. Not only that, people up there thought a lot of Justice Boney. They named a courthouse for him — Boney Courthouse. I wanted to see the courthouse.

But I am not here, at least in our journal of these travel jottings. Presently, we have just left Prince Rupert, the hotel with no air conditioning, but pretty good fans. I am glad they had those fans! Also, we didn't dump any coffee grounds in the sink as did the London ladies. In fact, we didn't even drink the coffee left in the room. We were trying to get away from there — wanting cooler atmospheres.

Some little side spots really got us into a good mood as we motored to a nearby place — Ksan. Ksan was an old native place adjoining the present town of Hazelton, British Columbia, Canada.

One of the main focus of interest for me was those totem poles. These totems carried a great significance for those natives. Still do. The totem was not just a pretty interesting piece of wood. These structurally imposing edifices have great meaning for the community. Not only physical in the terms of awe-inspiring art but the spiritual power claimed by the natives.

In each layer of the totem there is a characteristic underlying principle, motivation and sacredness in these carvings. Various animals were represented by courage, strength or judgment or discretion. In example, a badger could represent: determination, eagerness, strong will, focus, strategy, tenacity, defense, protection, independence and confidence. Each animal was accurately defined by the natives. We can see how much mental effort went into these characteristics — and the ones chosen.

After we left the grounds and the museum of Ksan we meandered through a path of dense foliage and found ourselves at the bank of the Skeena River. Through the ages Skeena River saw the gold seekers and the steamboats and earlier, the natives.

As I looked at one of the old steamboats I thought about Old Jacksonville, Ga. I thought of how those rear paddle kickers had brought prosperity to the Ocmulgee area as Skeena River brought prosperity to those pioneers.

Leaving we took a little bus ride and wound up at old Essington Port. Looking through the bus I started catching on-and-off glimpses of an old railroad — now forsaken. Earlier it had replaced the stately gallant steamboats and now neither existed in operation. Just like Old Jacksonville, Ga., the railroads had supplanted the steamboats. Then, like fury, Port Essington, with a diminishing population, was replaced with denser locations and more modern facilities and the place evaporated. Fires in the 1960s spelled the last flickers of living light and life of the old port.

But the old cannery is still there and we tourists come there to learn about the old history. It is interesting that they told us the salmon were sealed in cans and then the salmon were cooked. I thought of Russell. He probably thought we got him off on this trip, sealed him in that bus and cooked his goose. We hope he will find it in his heart, at least, some forgiveness. But it sure won't happen in Canada — or Alaska.

Credit: Geri-Gadder Tours of Bainbridge, Ga.; our fellow travelers; KY, IA, MO, SD, WY, MT, Canada info; Ksan info; personal experiences; personal info; other sources.

Totems have great meaning for the natives.

This one is at Ksan, Hazelton, British Columbia, Canada

When the steamboats of Old Jacksonville, Ga., were running, Canada had their steamboats in their rivers.

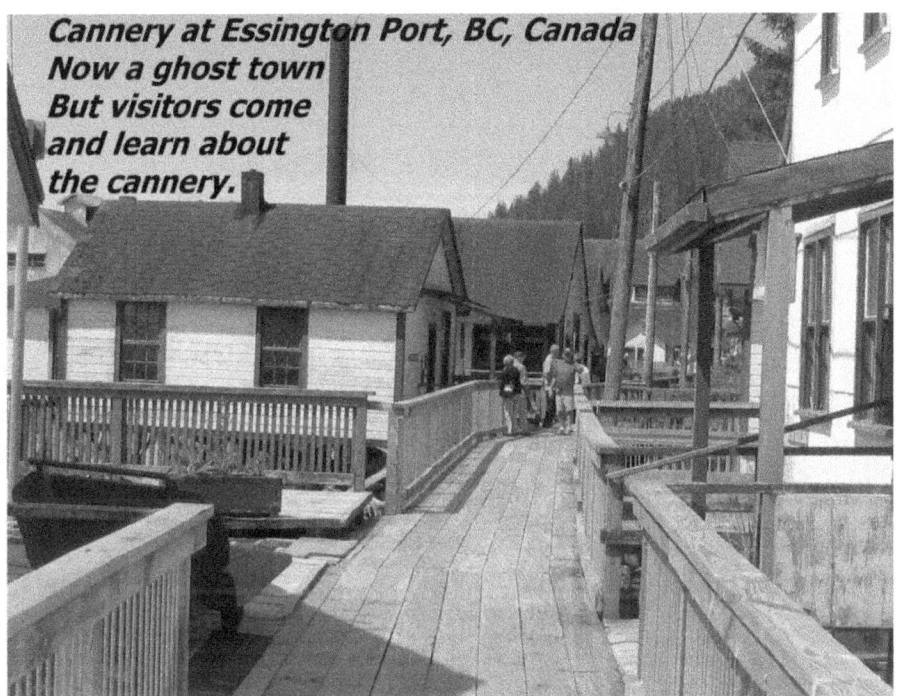

Cannery at Essington Port, BC, Canada Now a ghost town But visitors come and learn about the cannery.

Part 13
Ferry Takes Us To The "Inside Passage"

Well, the time had arrived. At Prince Rupert, BC, Canada, we were going to leave our bus and ride a ferry — to Alaska! Not really leaving our bus; actually we were going to take the bus with us — on the ferry! What a surprise! The ferry we encountered was not anything like the old ferries of the Ocmulgee River near Jacksonville, Georgia. Not by a long shot!

Russell Collins and I had the same thought. Is our big tour cruiser (bus) going to be able to fit into that ferry? As we neared the dock (terminal) we saw the big ferry (ship?). The large stern (rear) part of the ferry (ship) opened one of its huge doors and the lower inside vehicle deck revealed enough to get about 80 vehicles into that vessel. Our bus slowly rode into the yawning opening and our bus, and we, were on the ferry! Waterborne!

Getting out of the bus we went to an upper deck and received our keys for our cabin — lower berth and upper berth. Landlubbers would call those "bunk beds." In this article you will see a set of those berths just like the one assigned to Joanne and me. Joanne spent quite a bit of time in her lower berth as she proved to be a landlubber — not an old salt. The Inside Passage trip was not exactly peaceful in terms of her equilibrium and personal poise. In other words, she was not feeling very good at the moment (several moments). I felt very successful. I was able to climb that little red ladder to the top berth without breaking anything. And was able to reverse that to get out of the berth!

But, with the time-outs for off-center "sea legs" stability and mild sea sickness we were still able to clamber up to the cafeteria deck level where good food was served. Joanne and Grace especially liked the salmon and the halibut and we will talk more about those fishes later.

We were also able to get a little United States iced tea but Joanne had taken a liking for the sweetened Canadian tea. I am still wondering what fruit elixirs were mixed in that concoction cooked up by the

Canadians. But it was tasty. But it was also good to get some old-fashioned USA iced tea.

Not far off from Prince Rupert we began to steam northward to reach the United States, Alaska, and the port of Ketchikan — it came first of a series of towns for us (see map of picture).

We were now in the Inside Passage — a waterway — a mixture of mainland and islands that gave us a picturesque view of beautiful scenery and relative safety from the winds and turbulence of the open ocean just west. In these passages interspersed with islands and the mainland you might see anything. Another great ship (or ferry) passing, a small boat or vessel rowing through the fjords (fiords) to reach some distant destination for just the challenge of the course. Hardy men and women.

Or maybe an iceberg or a lofty mountain or a rustic seaport or a frolicking whale heaving its heavy tail upward and disappearing just before you could get a good shot of him (or her) with your camera! Again, you might get lucky.

It was interesting to talk with the people on the ferry. Some had cabins (sleeping berths) and others staked their personal areas by depositing their bodies in the couches or recliners in the observation deck. Others found other areas and wrapped up in blankets for the night (a short night). It was a sight.

As sundown approached the first day I got a good shot of an Alaskan setting in the Inside Passage. I faintly began to understand the beauty of this Last Frontier — God's creation. It was different. I hope the picture will be shown in color. But if it is not, just use your imagination. It is beautiful. Throw in some red and yellow and other colors. God let us see something pretty!

Credit: Geri-Gadder Tours of Bainbridge, Ga.; our fellow travelers; KY, IA, MO, SD, WY, MT, Canada, AK info; Inside Passage; personal experiences; personal info; other sources.

ALASKA
Little Diomede Island
RUSSIA
Nome
Yanrakynnot
Fairbanks
St. Matthew Island
Whittier
Anchorage
Valdez
College Fjord
Katmai National Park
Homer
Kayak Island
Kodiak
Skagway
CANADA
Haines
Juneau
Kake
Glacier Bay
Petersburg
Sitka
Wrangell
Ketchikan
Metlakatla
Pribilof Islands
Dutch Harbor
1st Port Ketchikan
Our Ferry "The Matanuska"
Vancouver
Seattle

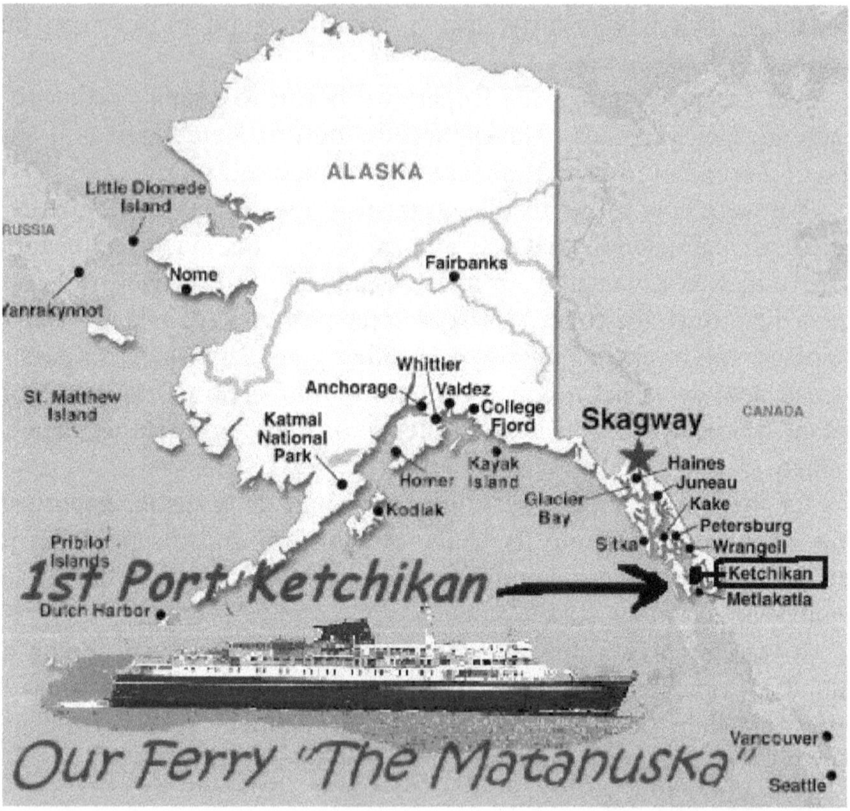

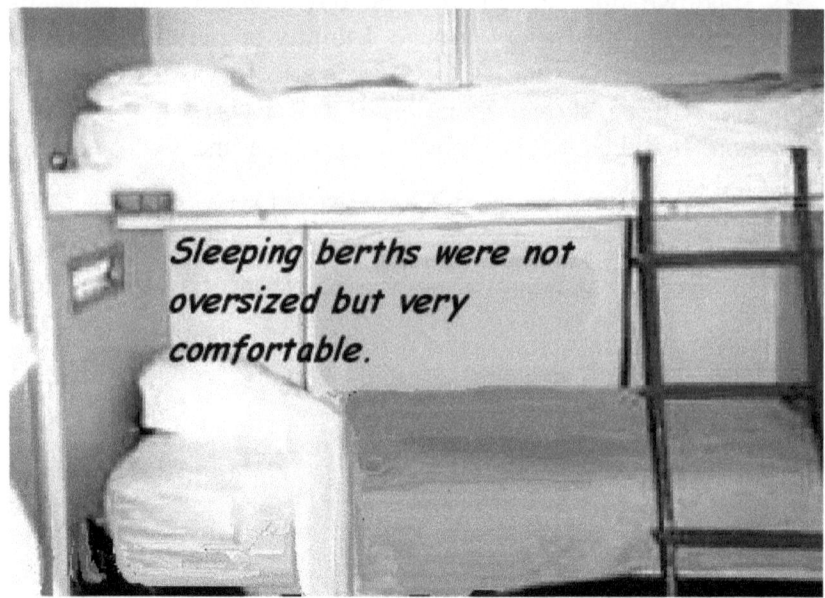

Sleeping berths were not oversized but very comfortable.

Part of the beauty of the Inside Passage

Part 14
Alaska's Cap'n "Hell Roaring Mike" Healy Came From Georgia

The Inside Passage is full of history. Approaching this long connecting islands/waterway, travelers are led from the "lower United States" to Alaska. All the seaport towns could chronicle events of rich histories.

We are still steaming along the Inside Passage and the noble ferry "Matanuska" is providing us with transportation, sleep, activity, viewing, eating and time to think and wonder. It is a good time to reflect. To learn more.

For instance, as we steamed near the old former Sitka, Alaska, capital we were reminded of some Georgia personalities who left deep and significant impressions. One man, Healy, hailed from Jones County, Georgia — near Gray and Macon. His family came to Georgia in 1823, the same time my Williams forefather came to Telfair County, Georgia, near Jacksonville, Ga. — with the Boney family. I am led to assume they came in 1823 for the same purpose — getting the lottery land when the Indians were pushed ever westward.

But Mr. Healy was a little different from most of the pioneers. Yes, he prospered greatly and had 49 slaves. But, unlike his neighbors, he took for his wife a slave lady of African-American identity. The couple remained dedicated and steadfast to their union and raised several children. Aware of their legal and cultural impositions and restrictions they immediately began to send each child to a northern school. To stay in Georgia would keep them in a slave status. They wound up at Holy Cross College — and became Catholics. In this atmosphere the children did not attract any identifying nomenclature concerning ethnic/racial identity. Except, for religion; they were Catholics — like most of the other students.

All the Healy children became prominent — a priest, bishop, rector, another a university president. The girls became nuns and one became a mother superior.

But there was one exception —Michael. Michael Healy was not of erudite bent; he was not inclined toward the academy. In other words, he did not want to go to school. Finally, escaping the ivy walls, he went to sea and became an expert in seamanship. His acute knowledge and application of the marine domain catapulted him into the captaincy.

Capt. Michael Healy was "Hell Roaring Mike." He ruled Alaska and brought order to sea and land. He brought swift justice to those who were wantonly killing sea otters, whales and innocent persons. He joined with missionary Sheldon Jackson and aided him in that work. He helped find food for starving natives. He helped Jackson start schools in Alaska. Someone said, "Who is Mike Healy?" The other replied, "He is the United States."

Capt. Mike Healy was the skipper of "The Bear" — the cutter flagship of the US Revenue/Coast Guard. With the ironclad hull the vessel stopped the most evil men of the high seas. Healy was feared and respected. He turned up when most unexpected. He got the job done.

Leaving Petersburg, looking at all those boats, not far from Sitka, I could imagine Mike Healy giving pursuit as he captured sea criminals.

As I thought about how much he had accomplished for Alaska and shaped that state I thought about his old home at Jones County, Georgia.

I thought about all the folks who had come from Georgia roots and had influenced other territories and states and nations. I even thought about Alaska Chief Justice George Boney and China Hill, Ga., near Jacksonville, Ga. I bet Justice Boney and Cap'n Mike would have made a good team fighting bad men. And, if they needed backup they could always call for Doc Holliday — another Georgian. It was good to see some of Georgia in Alaska.

Credit: Geri-Gadder Tours of Bainbridge, Ga.; our fellow travelers; KY, IA, MO, SD, WY, MT, Canada, AK info; Inside Passage; Capt. Michael Healy info and US Coast Guard; personal experiences; personal info; other sources.

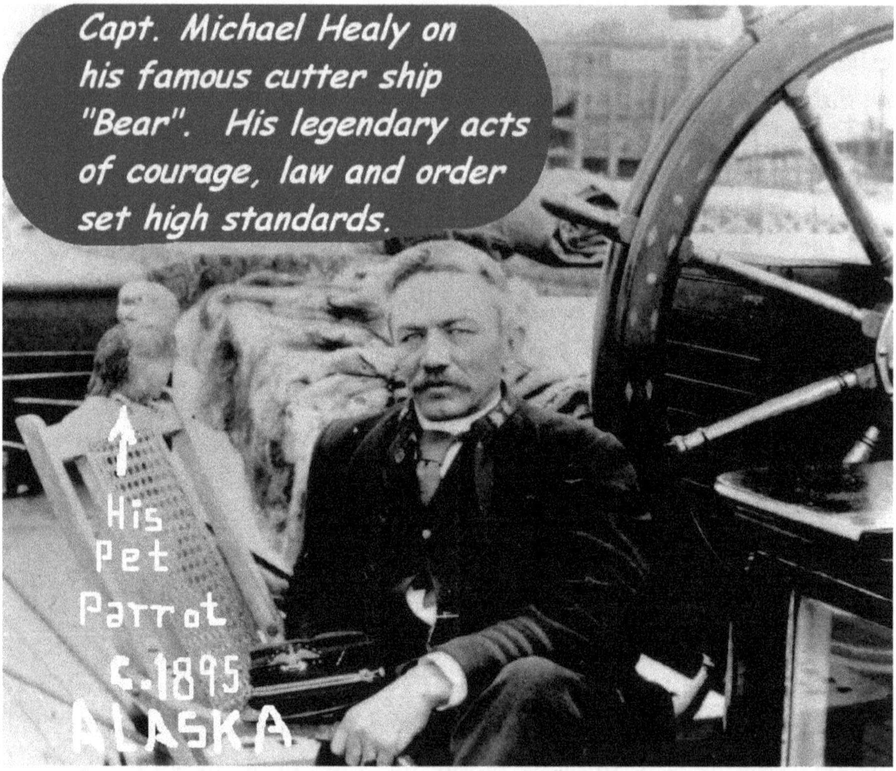
Capt. Michael Healy on
his famous cutter ship
"Bear". His legendary acts
of courage, law and order
set high standards.
His
Pet
Parrot
c.1895
ALASKA

Here we are at Petersburg, AK, Inside Passage.
People remember their old homelands, too.
Each year they celebrate "Norwegian Constitution Day".
They also do a lot of fishing !

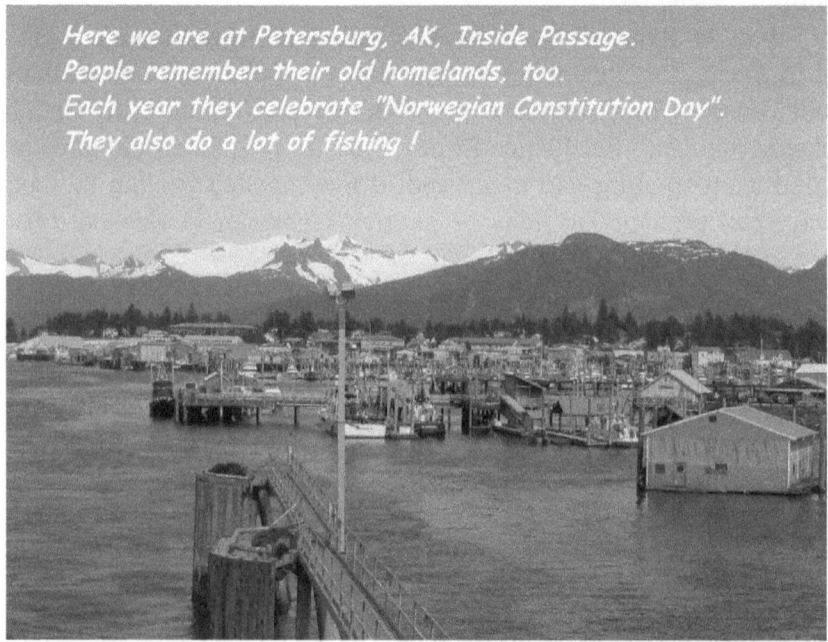

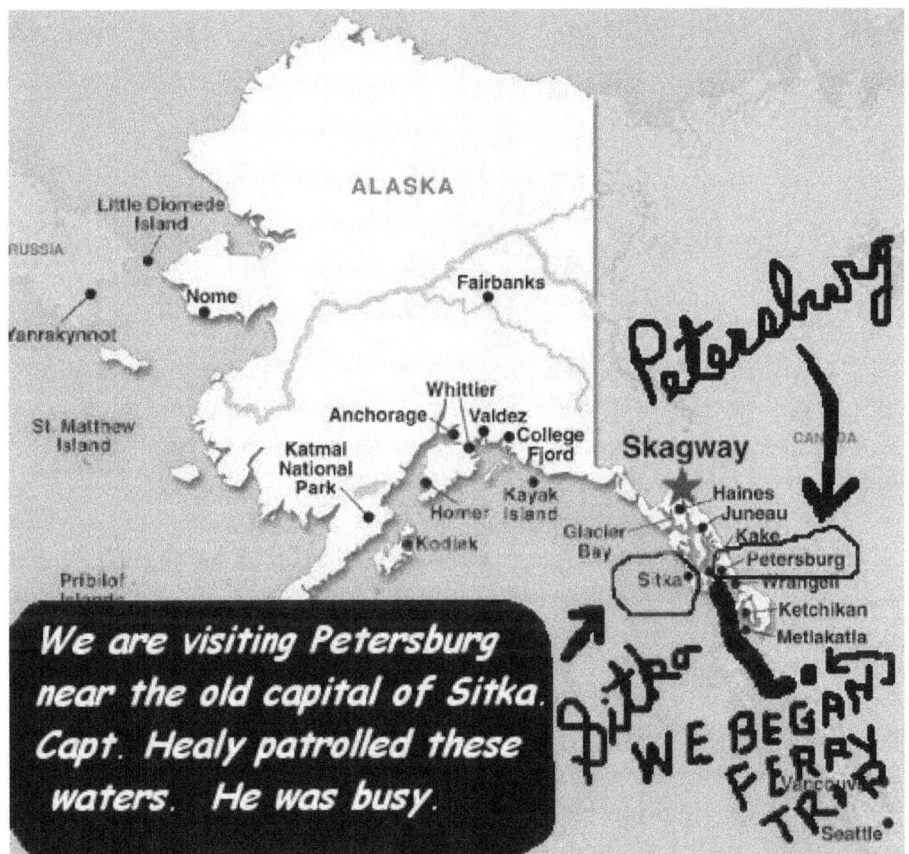

Part 15
Skagway Greeted Us With Friendly Faces, Old Tales And Cheap Goods

The Inside Passage was winding down. We were about to come alongside the pier and secure the lines and go ashore. Quickly we would break the seagoing routine of several hours, including two nights, and head for the colorful town of Skagway, Alaska.

Just before leaving our ferry, we took a picture on our port side (the left) where lay two huge luxury cruisers. It was interesting just to look at those splendid ships and compare those with our adequate and functional ferry, the noble and dependable — "The Matanuska." Although our old "Mat" did not compare with these modern marine leviathans the trusty and yeoman service of "Mat" proved to be good and faithful in its mission. It got us to Skagway. At just 408 feet long and puffing along at about 15-17 knots it made it! Hurrah!

As we boarded our bus in the hold of our ferry we took a long last view of the old ferry ship as we made contact with the connecting ramp heading for land. As we departed I wondered if we were the rats (undesirables) leaving the ship or if we were leaving the rats on the ship. I am sure Russell would vote for the latter. I gather Russell was not too keen about the Inside Passage "cruise."

You will have to go there to appreciate Skagway. The hustling bustling waves of people came like the waves of an ocean. To and fro the adults, youth and little ones zigzagged across the crowded streets and eagerly sought the best bargains in the many busy shops.

And, if you go there, buy your vacation junk at Skagway because its wares were good and very competitive. They were ready to sell and quickly — before these lunging crowds evaporated as they would board the railroad coaches nearby. Not that another thousands would quickly replace these but the merchants wanted the sale of this current customer. You could get a postcard for 15 cents and someone said another vendor had them for 10 cents. You could select from many Tshirts for only $1.99. It was a buyer's market.

Our female tour director, Glenda White (as opposed to Haskell, the male director), looked at each jewelry store in that village. She loves jewelry. Even if she just looks. I bet Haskell was nervous every time she went into those places. You will see her going across the street in one of these pictures in this article. Glenda was great and always made it a point to have our motel keys ready as we reached the lobbies. Haskell and Glenda worked hard to make our trip enjoyable. If interested you will see the tour listed in the credit.

Looking through the streets of Skagway, I had long lost Joanne, Grace and Russell and wound up at a building that I thought was a theater. I suppose it could be called that — it was a presentation of can-can ladies. One of the ladies was hanging out of the two-story building and I asked if I could take a picture. I thought the scene pretty well visualized this lively town! She was nice and told me I could take a picture and invited me to come inside for the presentation. I have to admit that I was a bit curious about what the can-can presentation consisted of but I was afraid I would miss the train if I lingered for this activity. I also knew Joanne, Grace and Russell would be upset with me if I saw the presentation and they missed it. So I took the picture and headed for the railroad.

But Skagway was and is an interesting town. So, next time, before I head for the train depot, I will tell you something else about Skagway.

Credit: Geri-Gadder Tours of Bainbridge, Ga.; our fellow travelers; KY, IA, MO, SD, WY, MT, Canada, AK info; Inside Passage; Skagway info; personal experiences; personal info; other sources.

We could not help but envy these great luxury cruise ships. But our old ferry "Mat" was reliable. It brought us to Skagway, Alaska. And, for a lots less expense!

Glenda, one of our tour directors, likes to visit the jewelry shops - if just to look!

This Can-Can girl allowed me to take a picture with my camera.

She was inviting us to come to the presentation.

Part 16
Skagway's Badman
"Soapy Smith" Was From Georgia

As I said, Skagway, Alaska, was and is an interesting town. In the late 1890s you were apt to see anything there — or anybody. You might even see, way back then, a Georgian. And up to now I have been able to report gallant and upstanding Georgia men going to Alaska — fighting crime and doing chivalrous things. But now we see a "bad onion." And this is not to reflect on the Red Onion Saloon but it seems it also had some nefarious conduct in that place. In other words, there was a lot of wickedness going on during the gold rush days.

And the leading gangster in Skagway was a Georgian! Jefferson R. "Soapy" Smith was born in Newnan, Georgia (Coweta County). Although the county's distinguished list includes Gov. Ellis Arnall, comedian Lewis Grizzard, Sheriff Lamar Potts and country singer Alan Jackson, "Soapy" Smith did not fit into any of those molds! Soapy was bad news. To the core. But, sometimes he did some good things!

Soapy got that name from one of his slick swindles — selling soap. He would do a sleight-of-hand and show a crowd a pile of soap. In this pile he would place a 50-dollar bill in the wrapper of the soap. And even a 100-dollar bill. Buyers getting the soap expected to hit a lucky pick and get one of those soap packets. They never did! Soapy would shuffle the soap and remove the moneyed soap! But to sweeten the temptation Soapy would introduce a "customer" (one of his outlaws) and the $50 would be in his soap. Then Soapy would excitedly say "there is another one in there and it is a $100 bill." Needless to say he plucked those gullible folks of a lot of money.

When Denver got too hot Soapy moved to Skagway and took over the town. He even had a telegraph installed and charged $5 for each transaction. Only problem — the wire only went to the wall. There was no operating telegraph — but the folks sending a wire to the states didn't know that. Soapy would even "receive" telegraph "messages" and relay those to waiting Skagway citizens. And those incoming messages were "collect" — so citizens had to pay on that end too!

Soapy got worse. Before long he owned the town and stole or illegally took goods or property and did other crimes, or had it done. But the crook was a smooth operator. While he was doing these unmentionables he was also helping the poor, safely escorting elderly widows to their homes, building churches and really showing a better side. His mixed motives kept both sides busy.

He even got President McKinley to help him get an Army unit going in Skagway — to help the effort of the Spanish-American War. Captain Soapy Smith would be allowed to drill his company in Ft. St. Michael, which was over 1,000 miles! That didn't bother Soapy at all. But he drilled his men at Skagway too and even personally placed his staff. His bartender was the military unit's chaplain!

But, the vigilantes of Skagway got tired of Soapy and his slick ways. Frank Reid told him not to trespass a guarded dock area. An altercation resulted and Soapy and Frank brought out guns and both were killed — Soapy immediately and Frank expired in 12 days. The town got back some respectability and order and Frank got a hero's monument in Gold Rush Cemetery. Still there. Soapy is in there too but his edifice is smaller.

Looking around all that history at Skagway I could just picture all that graft and mayhem. But I turned my attention to try to find Joanne, Grace and Russell. They are probably eating ice cream.

We made it to the train depot and Joanne and I posed with a couple of brown bears. But Bill Baab, former outdoor editor of *Augusta Chronicle*, corrected this illusion and had something like this to say: "Julian, those brown bears ain't live — because if they were — you would not be."

We liked Skagway but we heard the long whistle blow and it was time to get aboard the train that had taken many to the gold rush a century before. The engine took off with a jerk. Keep it on the rails! High mountains coming! It was exciting.

Credit: Geri-Gadder Tours of Bainbridge, Ga.; our fellow travelers; KY, IA, MO, SD, WY, MT, Canada, AK info; Skagway info; personal experiences; personal info; other sources.

*Jefferson R. "Soapy" Smith
(1860 - 1898)*

Part 17
Old Skagway Reminded Us Of Old Darien, Ga.

Please allow us to point out one Skagway place as the photo had to be removed from the article last week because of space. We are including it this week. If Russell will just tell the conductor to stop the train we can resume momentarily on that railroad excursion.

Backing up — The Red Onion Saloon at Skagway is important because the building and its events portray the very essence of the 1890s town. I am reminded of the old times of the Ocmulgee River area, Old Jacksonville, Ga. — right on to the Altamaha River and down to Darien, Ga., on the ocean. Of course, I was not there in 1898 but the old folks told us about what was going on. What was going on in Darien, Ga., was a parallel of what was going on in Skagway, Alaska, in 1898.

In Darien there were saloons, prostitutes, shady deals, downright theft, violence and murder and mayhem. It was the same scenery, at the same time, in Skagway, Alaska.

In Darien, some of the Ocmulgee River citizens would steer those long pines (logs) down the river. They would bind those long pine logs and form a timber raft and float the raft from Jacksonville, Ga., to Darien, Ga. Some of the sober types would sell their logs to an agent (some dishonest), get their money and make great haste back to Jacksonville. Those probably made a good amount of money. Others did not follow those routines. They would sell their logs, get their money, head out for a saloon, get drunk and before he could see the hazy fog dissipate in the early morning the victim had been separated from his money, usually either/or by a lady in waiting or somebody had rolled him. Today he would be called a mugger. Anyway, the victim would be without money, sick of whiskey and women and trying to figure the best way to get home.

In Skagway, the same picture. Gold miners who had worked hard like the raftsmen of Ocmulgee, headed from the hills to Skagway to get their gold changed to money. Then to the saloon, to the whiskey, to the women, and out on the street and out of money. Same song, different verse.

But, The Red Onion Saloon had a creative way of doing business. The bartender kept up with the transactions for the prostitutes and also informed each customer the status of each prostitute. The bartender did this by placing a doll, represented by each prostitute, on a rack near the bar. If the lady upstairs was busy with another customer the doll downstairs would be placed in the horizontal position. If the lady was looking for a customer the bartender would place the doll in the rack in the vertical position. By these two indicators the commerce would be kept moving and current. I wonder who came up with that method.

But, like the log rafts, the gold rush came to a stop. So, something had to replace the gold commerce. So some smart people came up with another solution — tourism!

They told us that a last census showed 862 permanent citizens in Skagway. But, the kicker is this — some 900,000 plus tourists in a year visit the quaint little town to see the history and all the shops. And they say in just a little time there would be over one million to come to Skagway and leave their money.

Skagway planned well. The sea outlet was directed so that huge cruiser ships could pull right up to the docks. And the little old train, the White Pass and Yukon Route, a narrow gauge railroad, which hauled miners to the gold fields, is used now to haul tourists. Of course, they had to add a few engines and coaches to satisfy the demand.

Now we can call Russell to tell the conductor to proceed with the train. We've got a lot of mountains to climb before this train reaches our bus. All aboard!

Credit: Geri-Gadder Tours of Bainbridge, Ga.; our fellow travelers; KY, IA, MO, SD, WY, MT, Canada, AK info; Skagway info; personal experiences; personal info; other sources.

This was the first brothel in Skagway in 1898. Dolls were used to signal the availability of the ladies of the night. Two indicators used - vertical and horizontal.

FROM THE LOOKS OF THIS OLD BUS IT HAS BEEN AROUND QUITE A WHILE. BUT THE VEHICLE WILL TAKE YOU TO "ALL POINTS OF INTEREST." SEEMS LIKE THE BUS IS FULL OF ANTICIPATING TRAVELERS.

This Dapper Gentleman might be dressing to convey the spirit of the town – The Young Couple invite us to a show.

Part 18
Skagway Train Rode Like Georgia's Old "Nancy Hanks"

When I rode from Jacksonville, Ga., in 1953, at the age of 13, to the Helena, Ga., I boarded an old train called "The Nancy Hanks." Seemed like half of Jacksonville was getting on that train to go to the Ponce de Leon Ball Park in Atlanta to see and hear Billy Graham. To see the great man of God was something to remember but at the same time, especially after we clunked back, noisily and jerkily, on The Nancy Hanks, I did not wish a repeat performance of that train. I would use some other conveyance to reach the arena of Rev. Graham. In the most remote place of my imagination did I think that I would ever get on that train or one like that.

I was wrong. In Skagway, Alaska, 2008, I boarded a very similar train. In fact, it looked about like it and it behaved just like it! That train — jerking along, careening from side to side, bumping, rumbling and emanating all the noises of the engine and the coaches — getting out of it every hiss, screech, banging inch!

We were on the White Pass/Yukon Railway just out of the antiquity of the latter 1890s and we knew it. It was now clicking along and started moaning and groaning as we tried to make those great steep climbs of the mountains, the tortuous curves and the doubtful bridges and trestles. Russell's eyes are usually a little squinted but now his eyes were big as jumbo or toebreaker marbles. My eyes were just as big. When I derailed I wanted to be sure I saw everything.

But this little narrow gauge railway formed in 1898 was important to Alaska. In those years it was important because it hauled gold miners to the Klondike. Miners had to get from Skagway to Dawson City and there was no road then. But the railroad was begotten at a great expense. Many men died as thousands of pounds of dynamite moved the mountains. With the rocks, from time to time, men came with it — to a falling death.

And the railroad had tough going. To begin with, Soapy Smith, the gangster we told you about, did not want the railroad started. But after Soapy was killed the effort moved quickly and the railroad was finished in record time.

As I looked, with big eyes, I witnessed all the places on the railway that looked like impossibilities. One trestle had a wooden lattice - high, very high. All that wood supported the railroad. I wondered how many trees it took to build that thing. We were way up there! And one of the pictures you see here lets you see just how high.

But they tell us the railroad started failing because the gold was slackening to a trickle and the economy would not hold up the railroad. In 1982 it ceased to be. But, not for long because smart men and women were thinking and came up with a great idea. The railroad could haul tourists from Skagway to the Canadian side and the tourists could review all the beautiful scenery and the gold rush history. It must have worked because thousands go there annually to get on that puffing little engine to get a load of history. Even the new coaches are crafted just like the old ones. In this way you can bump along in the same old historical railroad.

When we got off the train it was good to see our driver Kenny Gordon and his son Race Gordon. Our bus was a fine sight to see and we were glad to be back on it.

So, where are we going now? I bet we are heading for some nice motel to rest in comfort and I bet Russell cannot wait to see it!

Credit: Geri-Gadder Tours of Bainbridge, Ga.; our fellow travelers; KY, IA, MO, SD, WY, MT, Canada, AK info; Skagway info; personal experiences; personal info; other sources.

Part 19
Gold Fields Were Unforgiving But Yukon Is Breathtaking

Leaving our train we again gained possession of our tour bus. Riding away from the old train brought mental images of what those crusty old pioneers looked like in 1898. As they ascended those hills in the train and on foot they had to carry 1,000 pounds of supplies. The government required gold miners and others to carry a lot of food, tools and other necessaries because they knew it would be suicide to do otherwise. The Yukon and the Klondike gold fields were unforgiving.

And there were about as many "fast money" con-men as there were legitimate men making claims and working the gold. Too many criminals were covering the territory seeking to steal claims, gold and money. Some second-thinking aspirants gave up the ghost quickly as they thought about the great physical effort of hauling half a ton of supplies plus many hazards — bad weather, bad animals, bad humans and bad luck! They also figured in the equation that also might include no gold being discovered. Those cowering at those odds adjusted by becoming businessmen at one of the forming towns and became profitable by selling picks, pans, food items and other things.

And women came. Some sought to marry a gold miner. Some came to administer the healing arts. Others, kindly called "the ladies of the night," came to attract flesh when that became weak. Everyone was out to make money.

But as we drove, this whispering history lost its telling and the chattering of our bus friends became dominant. We were seeing some beautiful scenery. I got so excited that I could not take a passable picture. Joanne got a kick out of my frustration and finally offered to take a presentable picture. But her effort was more than average camera taking. I had to admit that Joanne took the best image I saw in the whole time — especially given that we were moving and the foliage kept getting in the way. But she hit the button at the precisely correct time and her result is included with this article. As you can see by this image — the lake, little island, greenery, mountains and sky - it was perfect.

Of course, this little photographic event, which had deteriorated to a contest, caused me no small troubles as Russell kept reminding me that I could not take good pictures but Joanne could. Realizing it was a lost cause I also relented and let Joanne or someone else take the fine picture of the Dall sheep even though he was stuffed or made of plastic. Secondary to the Dall sheep, Russell, J.L. and I are also posed. We wanted to have a picture of all of us in case we fell off the mountain or ran into a real angry Dall sheep. Looks more like a goat. And you can never know, especially in the part of this country we were seeing. We had never seen the likes of all the possibilities the Yukon possessed. Liable to see anything here.

Speaking of entering Yukon we were entering this beautiful, rugged and diverse sector residing in Canada. Russell, Grace, Joanne and I could not resist getting our picture taken by the big Yukon sign. I'll bet a lot of folks have posed by that sign. You could see the ruts left from people coming and going to that tourist attraction.

As the bus flew by we thought we were enjoying mountain ash, white spruce, birch, poplar, aspen, and pine but all we really knew - these trees were green. Lots of green. It was beautiful. And I think I was sure of the poplar and the pine.

We are now heading for the town of Whitehorse and with a name like that there must be a story there.

Credit: Geri-Gadder Tours of Bainbridge, Ga.; our fellow travelers; KY, IA, MO, SD, WY, MT, Canada, AK info; Yukon info; personal experiences; personal info; other sources.

Part 20
Earthquake, Sea Otters
And A July "Merry Christmas"

If you will permit us to fast-forward we are going to leave Whitehorse on the Yukon, and go to Valdez, Alaska, because we are almost staring right at Christmas! And Valdez and the adjacent Prince William Sound will get us in the mood for Christmas! Get ready for a cool environment. Grab a coat! We are going to board the beautiful Lu-Lu Belle boat for a whole day's excursion — water animals, icebergs, a great glacier (Columbia), and colorful and strange birds.

But peering through the bus's windows Russell and I, and some of the other folks, were not quite as concerned about reaching our waiting adventuresome boat Lu-Lu Belle as we were concerned about another little tidbit of information that emerged from our trip itinerary. This little statement was something like this: "Welcome to the beautiful Valdez, AK. The town was completed erased from existence by an earthquake and tsunami in 1964." To make it worse this was added: "The magnificent scenery — will keep you spell-bound all the way to Valdez." Russell and I were spell-bound but it concerned some of the risks of this place. The following words did not do anything to assuage our fears: "As we arrive in Valdez, there is very little evidence that Valdez was virtually destroyed in the 1964 earthquake." It sounded like to Russell and me that they were trying to cover it up! This last statement certainly confirmed our worst anxieties — "We spend the night here." You can imagine our quality of sleep while imagining every rumble from wherever was another bad earthquake! Horrors, how did we get into this place?!

But by the time we reached our dock slip the view of the great Lu-Lu Belle massaged every tense nerve and caused us to look with great anticipation toward becoming "mates" of the Lu-Lu Belle. Captain Fred Rodolph immediately calmed our minds and reservations and we knew we were in for a great time.

As we slowly left our slip and headed for open sea I could tell

Cap'n Fred and Lu-Lu Belle were quite a few knots better than par. After we got through the protected paddling sea otters Cap'n Fred relaxed, fixed his instruments for steaming and started telling us stories as good as some of those yarned by old-timers of Old Jacksonville, Ga. This Cap'n Fred was a masterful talker. And if you ever want to get a boat in Prince William Sound you would do no better than to look up Cap'n Fred.

I made it my business to go up to the bridge with Cap'n Fred as he earnestly loves for people to come up there. He will give you enough commentary to last you a long time. And he is interesting - not to say that he is also probably one of the most knowledgeable persons in those waters, if not the best.

And down below Cap'n Fred's staff will make sure you are comfortable and have something to eat. You can get something up there anytime. As long as you have some money. Tourism goes right along with extracting a reasonable amount of currency. I suppose it is why it works so well. Alaska is waiting for the money and the tourists are trying to get there to give them money.

But, we will try to talk more about this excursion in another article. And, just now one of those big whales jumped and is disappearing in the water. Hope he doesn't surface under "Lu-Lu Belle" (our boat)!

By the way, Lu-Lu Belle and staff even photographed our couples with "Merry Christmas." And today, we would also like to wish you a "Merry Christmas." And remember this about Christmas. The real Christmas! It was not an accident. You can count on that!

Credit: Geri-Gadder Tours of Bainbridge, Ga.; our fellow travelers; KY, IA, MO, SD, WY, MT, Canada, AK info; Valdez and Prince William Sound info; personal experiences; personal info; other sources.

"Lu-Lu Belle" Our Boat

It's Mighty COOL For The Middle Of The Summer!

Grace & Russell

Part 21
Sea Otters Were Slaughtered To Brink Of Extinction But Now Protected

Well, we were not able to get the picture of our noble boat "Lu-Lu Belle" in the paper last week (but now in the book) because we were a little bit squeezed for space. But, if things go well the paper can include the image in this week and it will perfectly fit as we continue probing around in the icebergs and whales and many other things.

As I questioned Cap'n Fred, skipper of the Lu-Lu Belle, I asked him how deep it was in one of the areas in Prince William Sound. That was easy for Cap'n Fred because he just checked his depth finder or whatever he called it and told me our depth at that spot was 750 feet. I told him that was deep enough to suit me! I could tell that Russell thought that was way too deep.

But, of all the animals, we found the little sea otters most interesting and different. In fact, we became fascinated with all the water animals. Looking at the sea otters they could cling together closely and the mothers and pups seemed to be inseparable. They seemed to hold the bottoms of their feet elevated in the air to keep that part out of the water. But those pads on the front feet could do many things — including pounding clams and mussels and related "hard-shells" with rocks cradled around these pads. The little sea otters were using a tool to gain entrance to their food! I suppose it takes a pretty smart animal to be able to use tools.

But the difference in the sea otters also became a liability for these cute little creatures. After the mid-1700s the Russians began to go into the area of what is known as Alaska; they found that the high quality of fur of the sea otter could not be equaled in other animals.

The Russians began such a frenzied pursuit of these little creatures that they almost erased the whole sea otter population! Someone told me that the estimated 200,000 to 300,000 sea otters came perilously close to nonexistence — only 1,000 or 2,000 sea otters left!

In fact, the Russians were so greedy about killing these sea otters, they were even killing the native Aleuts — kidnapping, extorting and even killing the natives as the Russians forced the natives to hunt the otters.

As I ran my fingers over a sample swatch in one of the park museums I began to realize the allurement and desire for this little creature. About all of the animals were exhibited on the display board but only the sea otter was so fine and exquisite and superior. On that square inch sample there were about one million hairs on that small area. To touch the fur told you instantly why the poachers and killers would do anything to get those furs.

For awhile after America took over the territory in 1867 there were efforts to reestablish the sea otter population. Then over-hunting took over and it was not until recently that the sea otter came into protected status. In this status the population is quickly regaining almost its past numbers.

Someone said this little fellow, the sea otter, is a member of the weasel family and maybe a distant relative of a beaver. But whatever he is I will have to say he is what my Workmore School teacher Mrs. Ashley called, "stickability." By the way, this is not what I was but what Mrs. Ashley desired me to be.

We were funning about Russell Collins and getting enough of the Lu-Lu Belle and all it consisted of — and sending out an SOS flag. But, we are convinced of this — if he could have gotten ahold of an SOS flag he would have flown it.

It seems such a pity because the picture with the man holding the flag looks just like Russell!

Maybe by the time we get closer to the cliffs by the sea Russell will take a greater appreciation of wildlife when he sees those birds called "puffins." They are weird looking birds!

Credit: Geri-Gadder Tours of Bainbridge, Ga.; our fellow travelers; KY, IA, MO, SD, WY, MT, Canada, AK info; Valdez and Prince William Sound info; personal experiences; personal info; other sources.

We Enjoyed Alaska – But Russell Just About Killed Us!

These sea otters seem to be relaxing. Not at all like past years - when the little creatures were killed for their fur. Now they are protected.

Russell thinks the boat is just a mite too close to the glacier and the icebergs.

Iceberg

Glacier

Julian Joanne Grace Russell

Part 22
Puffins, Seals And Whales Put On Quite A Show

The long trip out to Prince William Sound must be getting to us. From our eyes we are seeing some strange things. For example, some of these birds. Especially, a little bird they call a "puffin."

At first, we rubbed our eyes as we could hardly believe this bird. His head looked like a parrot but his feet looked like a duck! Beautiful too and many colors — yellow, orange, black, blue and white. The puffin's gaudy attire was more striking than the Oregon Ducks football team! I also found those little puffins could operate about as well as those Oregon Ducks.

I would have dearly liked taking a few of those puffins back to Old Jacksonville, Ga., but by the way those Canadian guards inspected Russell I was afraid to try it. Because we were going to have to go back that way and it was no way to evade the Royal Canadian Mounties.

In fact, later we wound up in the very headquarters of the Mounties! Watched some of the recruits working out. Now, we will have to tell you something more about all that but we are skipping other things now so we will put that on hold.

Some of the natives told us these puffins behaved a lot like geese — when it came to mating. Of course we have been told for a long time that geese mated for life. Stayed together with their original mates. The Alaskans told us that puffins do the same.

But these puffins do a little different with some things. I suppose we didn't see any really little puffins because they were way down in a burrow. Light hurts these little fellows and this deep burrow also protects them from enemies.

And daddy puffin and mama puffin diligently tend to this one baby. When one parent looks for food the other will keep the baby under wing. They will keep him for quite a time, feeding him as much as 10 times each day.

But, things change! When the "puffling" is big enough the parents abandon the burrow and leave him! He has to get out of the burrow and look for food. Unfortunately, sometimes he heads for land (or a town!) and gets into big trouble! Sometimes town children will try to catch them and set them toward the sea but many times rats, foxes, black gulls and other varmints make these pufflings into a meal.

But these Alaska folks think a lot of these puffins and pufflings. We stayed in one hotel and it is called "The Puffin."

We also enjoyed all those seals in and around the Prince William Sound. To see one out in the sea perched on an iceberg he looks pretty spiffy. But we found pretty quickly that a bunch of seals lounging at the base of the cliffs resulted in some stiff (stinking) winds! Like the fellow who told colleagues who were complaining about someone's deodorant — "It can't be me — I don't use any." I don't believe those seals used any deodorant!

And we can't leave out those great whales that jumped and flipped and entertained us with great effort and showmanship and performance.

I hate to think what would have happened if one of those leviathans had landed on our boat "Lu-Lu Belle." That would have been a mess.

It would have also damaged one of the most beautiful boats I have seen. Cap'n Fred built it himself. If you think outstanding workmanship is something that is gone with the wind just stroll down to Cap'n Fred's dock slip. You will see why he is proud of his masterpiece! Truly a piece of work!

Credit: Geri-Gadder Tours of Bainbridge, Ga.; our fellow travelers; KY, IA, MO, SD, WY, MT, Canada, AK info; Valdez and Prince William Sound info; personal experiences; personal info; other sources.

We Enjoyed Alaska – But Russell Just About Killed Us!

Part 23
Wooly Mammoths And Wolverines Looked Ready For War

Our detour to the icebergs was to get the Christmas theme together and be able to give you a "Merry Christmas" sign that was provided by our boat "Lu-Lu Belle." Cap'n Fred took great pains to have everything just as it should. He personally built the excursion boat which is a piece of solid, elegant and appealing craft — very high quality. He is proud of the boat and should be.

I suspect that old Captain John L. Day of the steamboat days of the Ocmulgee River was of the same ilk of Cap'n Fred and practiced this same good craftsmanship. One old timer once described one of his steamboats and it sounds like Cap'n Day had a fine steamboat going to Old Jacksonville, Ga., and other points. In fact, he made several steamboats.

Later we will touch on the Christmas theme again when we reach the North Pole but we will hold off on that until we get there. Right now we return to our departing train, getting on the tour bus and heading for Whitehorse, Yukon, Canada.

As I suspected there was a tale behind that name, Whitehorse. One of the natives said Whitehorse is called that because some rapids on the water nearby looked like a white horse's mane and so they called the place Whitehorse. Another person said some Indian named Whitehorse came along and drowned in the water and they labeled the town in honor of that ancestor. Either makes a good tale; nevertheless, the town is still called Whitehorse. Way back it was called White Horse but when it took the capital of Yukon away from Dawson City in 1953 it became one word — Whitehorse.

On the way to Whitehorse we went into a museum and found some interesting animals. One animal, long gone, the wooly mammoth, was there as a replica to give us a good idea of what he looked like. This picture we took in the museum tells us the wooly mammoth was huge. Some info said the wooly mammoth forked off from an elephant about one million and a half years! I don't know how they tell that because possibly none of us were around to report that phenomenon and I don't think any of those possible reporters left any reports. But I would fear one if he stepped on my foot; those creatures were immense. But now extinct.

But, people are smart. I noticed in a pharmacy store that they claim your pictures on the CD (Compact Disc) will hold up for 100 years. Have you thought — CDs have not been tested for 100 years and nobody has been testing those for 100 years? But, anyway, maybe these pictures will hold up until we can get them to the paper (and to this book).

Browsing around in this museum I found another unusual animal, at least for us — the wolverine. Look at the picture here — if you believe that little item is able to defend himself you are probably right! Somebody up there in Alaska told me the wolverine is something you don't want to mess with! He even has a tooth that swings out to 90 degrees (sideways) and can tear and rip about anything with that. He is another one of those weasels and is about the size of a usual medium dog. His hair is thick and his ferocious teeth and sharp claws back him up pretty well. And he is very strong. Someone said the wolverine will not even back up from a bear if it becomes necessary. He doesn't smell like perfume either — hence, his name, "nasty cat." Bad fellow.

As far as I can tell, right here at the museum, I believe I just want to look at him eyeball to eyeball — right here at the museum. If he was looking for me I would be like Ken Vickers of *Cracklin' Bread* — I would like to put as much distance and duration between ole wolverine and me as possible!

Joanne, my wife, is looking at the Whitehorse sign and we will be getting there soon. I sure want to see that steamboat!

Credit: Geri-Gadder Tours of Bainbridge, Ga.; our fellow travelers; KY, IA, MO, SD, WY, MT, Canada, AK info; Whitehorse and Yukon info; personal experiences; personal info; other sources.

We Enjoyed Alaska – But Russell Just About Killed Us!

Back in Canada - Yukon - Klondike
"way back to them thar' hills of GOLD!" Joanne

I told Russell I didn't think we could pet this little animal -- he is a wolverine and probably more like a cross between a wildcat and an alligator! They said he was real mean!

Part 24
Muskox Visit And "Steamboat Fever" Made A Big Day

I got back on the bus and we headed for Whitehorse, Yukon, Canada, but I could not forget one of the animals back there at the museum. In fact, there were three — a mama, a baby and a papa — muskoxen or simply, muskox. And to confuse me they told me the muskox was not really an ox. They said he belonged to the sheep and goats!

In fact, I really didn't believe an animal could be walking around (alive) that resembled that creature I had been looking at. But those native people kept telling me that the muskox was just as alive as that bear and moose we had seen. I would have to see this muskox in a living breathing form before I would believe it. Why? This muskox looked more like something that existed with that wooly mammoth. And my museum guide agreed.

But, my guide said the muskox somehow escaped and did not perish with other prehistoric animals. And the guide said I would probably see a living sample of the muskox because tour directors usually take tourists to a farm having some muskoxen. I still couldn't believe it.

But, in a little while — sure enough. We reached a place and the director took us to a farm and out in the field was a muskox — in fact, several of those. What a sight! I thought I was looking at a creature that took me back to 200,000 years! I marveled at that animal — that he represented an animal that had an unbroken lineage for those many many years.

I hope the muskox will stay. In fact, he was killed out in Alaska but he was reintroduced by other muskox from other places in Canada and he is doing good. I hope my grandchildren will get to see the muskox — and their grandchildren.

Why, if we could get a couple of muskox, maybe a herd, in Old Jacksonville, Ga., we would have an exhibit that would be the envy of all. But I don't suppose they would live here. They said the weather might get down to around 16 degrees this weekend. The muskox would love that.

But, just around the bend, at Whitehorse, I would temporarily forget the muskoxen. Standing before me in its stately and imposing beauty and strength was S.S. Klondike — the steamboat!

Would I be permitted to go aboard this magnificent steamboat? Visions of the old Ocmulgee River sternwheelers danced in my mind of long gone lore — of hardworking men hoisting barrels of tar and bales of cotton, of a hard captain instructing a crew member about checking the boiler, a lady and gentleman coming aboard for their long-awaited honeymoon on the river, the mournful tones of the whistle departing, and the sight of a brawny sailor throwing off the last line from the dock.

Before I knew it we were heading for The Klondike and we were going aboard. A young lady escorted us around the great boat. Below deck we could see and handle the complicated valves and gauges that held lives in safety — or danger! We remembered the strength and weakness of river men — steamboat fever! Steamboat fever would sometimes overtake good men and they would push their vessels to a breaking point — to defeat an opponent in a steamboat race! Unfortunately, sometimes the result was — steamboat explosion!

We saw the little cabins on the upper deck that were the bedrooms of the passengers of the steamboat. No wasted space there.

And still higher we saw the pilot house — the bridge — the captain's wheel. As I held onto this great wheel I could only imagine the responsibility of that captain. Only my picture can convey my emotions. Surely, I was almost overtaken by steamboat fever. I was as happy as Davy Crockett at Congress when General John E. Coffee of Jacksonville, Ga., told him that a steamboat had been named for "David Crockett" on the Ocmulgee River. Davy gave Gen. Coffee some banners to signify the name of the steamboat - "David Crockett." And the Ocmulgee River steamboat captain was glad to get those flags. Steamboat Fever!

Credit: Geri-Gadder Tours of Bainbridge, Ga.; our fellow travelers; KY, IA, MO, SD, WY, MT, Canada, AK info; Whitehorse and Yukon info; personal experiences; personal info; other sources.

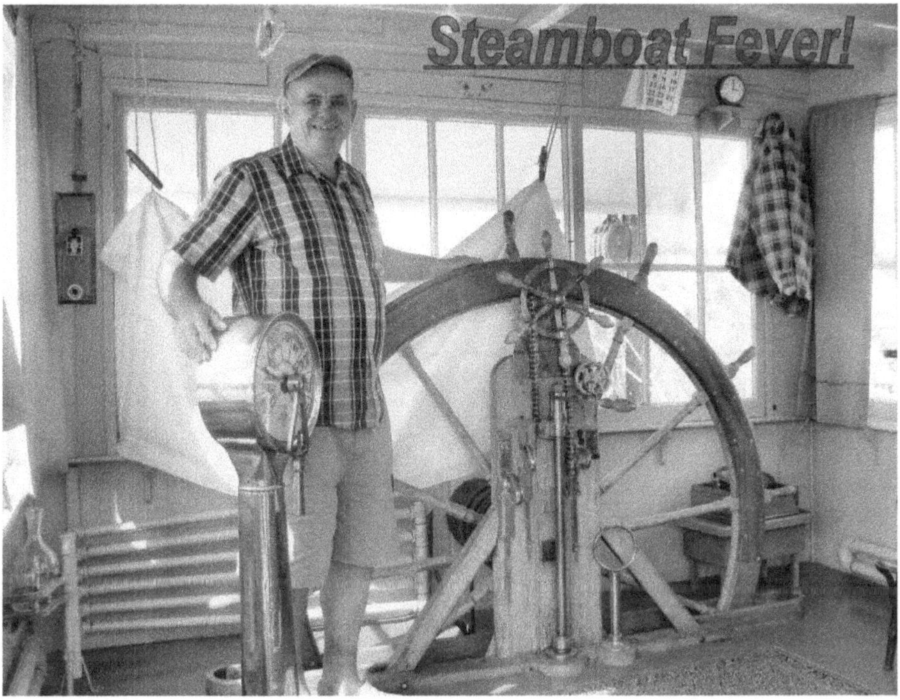
Steamboat Fever!

"Black Swan"
Hawkinsville
Georgia

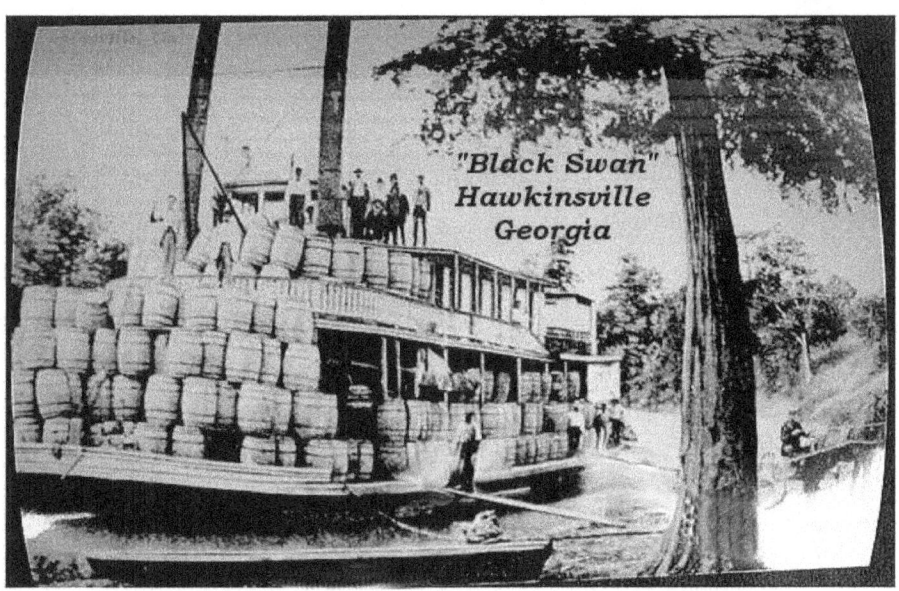

Part 25
Tiny Motel Room, Big Smart Dog
And Russell Made A Crowd

Trying to get from Whitehorse to Dawson City is like trying to put eight slick eels in a croaker sack. If you ever got an order from someone wanting several eels from trotlines (at night) in the Ocmulgee River then you can relate. Those eight eels were more trouble than the whole 67 pounds of catfish we caught that night. I had just about fool with a gar than mess with an eel. But I don't believe anyone ever ordered any gar.

But, first, we've got to get our muskoxen and the steamboat pictures in this section because those images are better than any descriptions. And here they are. We certainly don't have anything in Georgia that looks like these muskoxen!

Now, the present task is to get Russell to calm down a bit because I will have to agree with him, the lodging opportunities are narrowing drastically about now. Now, Russell might want you to believe the pictured motel is for real but to be truthful the motel was just a bit better than this building. But this building would be big enough to move around. The real motel was quite compact. We won't reveal this one because we don't want to be sued.

Unfortunately, at about twelve midnight, as I tried to reach from my bed to the bathroom I suddenly found myself on the floor — or rather, in the suitcase! The room was so small we had to put the suitcase between the bed and the bathroom. I think I heard Russell holler down the hall about the same time because I don't think they were placed in the honeymoon suite this time. In fact, I don't think that motel had a honeymoon suite. I bet Russell fell in his suitcase too. Or it might have been Grace's.

Russell was having a bad time at the motel. About the only bright event this stop was when we walked to the general store to buy odds and ends for supper and breakfast. Right now the restaurants were scarce so we looked for Vienna sausages, crackers, fruit cups and Pepsi.

And, I forgot too, we also had an opportunity to get in some walking. But I don't think Russell likes to walk. He also gets on to me about parking too far from the restaurants. I told him the main thing is — exercise. Russell said he thought he would have me committed.

But, now, back at the motel, was the last straw. Russell ran into this large white dog in the motel office. I could tell right off Russell and the dog did not like each other. I think the large white dog was the same one I saw sitting in the driver's seat in the truck — and moving the steering wheel; fortunately, the truck was not moving. But I could tell that was a smart dog. Any dog attempting to perform maneuvers with a steering wheel needs to be watched.

I tried to keep a close watch on Russell and the white dog because I certainly did not want any trouble at that little motel. It didn't take many to get a crowd gathered in this little motel. And we had already reached a crowd. Time to move to the bus and depart.

As you look at Russell and the large white dog you will understand why I said the dog was smart and for Russell to leave him alone. Fortunately, they wound up in a stalemate. Deadlocked — staring. All ended well.

I still remember that white dog. I still believe he changed the TV channel in the motel office with that remote. Smart dog. But Russell and I had stayed a little bit ahead of the game and we intended to do just that — for the duration of the days of Canada and Alaska!

Credit: Geri-Gadder Tours of Bainbridge, Ga.; our fellow travelers; KY, IA, MO, SD, WY, MT, Canada, AK info; Whitehorse and Yukon info; personal experiences; personal info; other sources.

We Enjoyed Alaska – But Russell Just About Killed Us!

Living Vestiges of a Prehistoric Age

S.S. Klondike Steamboat

Russell has just found a "No Smoking" room with a nice motel and plenty of water (if the wind will move the windmill).

MOTEL

PS - Just Kidding - We always had running hot & cold water!

DELUXE EXTERIOR BATH-ROOM

Russell mentioned something about "Georgia, Georgia." I think he was singing.

Part 26
Steamboats Hold Some Strange Tales

Two old steamboats — one near Jacksonville, Ga., and one in The Yukon Territory — in an indirect way had something in common. Freezing and burning.

Freezing and burning. We have heard it — "I am freezing to death — turn up the heat." But one old timer gold miner in The Yukon once carried this expression to the extreme. Sam McGee was so cold he wanted to be cremated when his time came to cash in his chips.

And right now, we are leaving Whitehorse and heading for Dawson City for a piece of that action. Somewhere between those towns a famous lake — the Lake Laberge (Lebarge) — was the said lake of where Sam McGee was deposited for his fiery interment. In an old steamboat. He also deposited some money in the bank which is coming next.

And, at the Commerce Bank of Dawson City we will be able to photograph that famous bank — once inhabited by the famous poet of Robert Service. Actually, Mr. Service was a good banker and worked there. But, between loans and handling cash and checks he wrote poems and no one seemed to care that he did that. In fact, it seems somebody even encouraged his bent for composing words.

It was at the bank that he encountered a man called Sam McGee, a customer. And at about the same time Mr. Service also heard about a strange thing — an old miner who had asked a friend to cremate him at his death.

Poet Robert Service knew a good story when he saw it. He asked Sam McGee if he could use his name — because his last name rhymed with "Tennessee." His first (and last) stanza of his poem went like this:

"There are strange things done in the midnight sun
By the men who moil for gold;
The Arctic trails have their secret tales
That would make your blood run cold;

The Northern Lights have seen queer sights,
But the queerest they ever did see
Was that night on the marge of Lake Lebarge
I cremated Sam McGee."

The temperament of Sam was a little short of loving this area of cold and desolation. He and Russell, our trip colleague, had about the same disposition concerning all of this:

"Now Sam McGee was from Tennessee, where the cotton blooms and blows.
Why he left his home in the South to roam 'round the Pole, God only knows.
He was always cold, but the land of gold seemed to hold him like a spell;
Though he'd often say in his homely way that "he'd sooner live in hell."

Sam hated the cold so much he really wanted to be cremated so he could be warm! Even hot. The poet even told of Sam being in the boiler (a steamboat used to burn his remains). But, here Sam is happy in the blazing boiler:

"And there sat Sam, looking cool and calm, in the heart of the furnace roar;
And he wore a smile you could see a mile, and said: "Please close that door.
It's fine in here, but I greatly fear, you'll let in the cold and storm —
Since I left Plumtree, down in Tennessee, it's the first time I've been warm."

So an old steamboat was used to put frozen Sam away in a furnace. And between Jacksonville, Ga., and Lumber City, Ga., an old steamboat captain (late) was put away in a frozen grave. But, like Sam, the old Captain's adopted son stayed by that frozen grave until it got hot enough to dig the grave, thaw everything out and bury the waiting Captain.

Old steamboats have a lot of tales. Some true, some not, but most of the time there is enough truth there to merit the telling.

By the way, if you want to read the whole poem, click Google and write in "The Cremation of Sam McGee." Quite a tale.

Credit: Geri-Gadder Tours of Bainbridge, Ga.; our fellow travelers; KY, IA, MO, SD, WY, MT, Canada, AK info; Whitehorse, Dawson City and Yukon info; personal experiences; personal info; other sources.

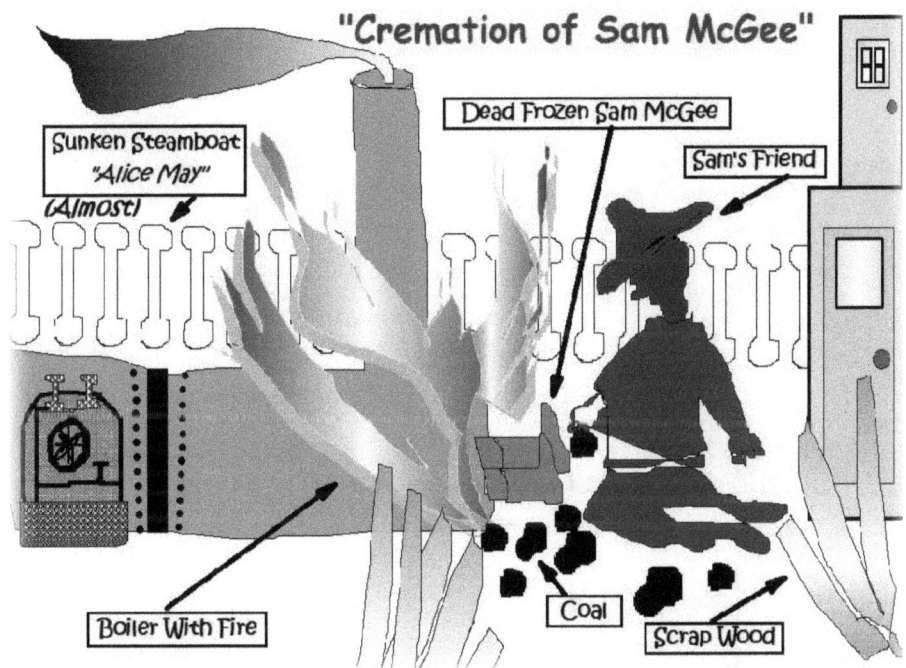

Poet Robert Service who wrote "The Cremation of Sam McGee" worked at this bank in Dawson City at one time.

HIS CABIN

Part 27
Mounties Tried To Protect Crazy Gold Seekers

After we left the surroundings of Lake Laberge (Lebarge) we could still picture Sam McGee stuck in the old derelict steamboat in the lake — being cremated. The graphic illustration just reminded us how many old miners met dangers on every turn. We are now trying to get to Dawson City and like the old miners it seemed to be pretty tough getting there. Even for us — if you are traveling on a bus. For example, if anyone in our group fell into one of those roadside potty stations he or she would be a long gone person. Dark down in there and it seemed to be deep. If you holler down in there your echo does not even come back! And perched on some side of a high mountain. Forbid that we ever have a landslide!

But after we visited the restroom relief station we were gone again toward Dawson City. As I looked at the mountains and the rivers I knew those Gold Rush participants had a rough time. Some tried to get to Dawson City by various routes.

The ones, the majority, tried to get to Skagway, cross the Chilkoot Pass or White Pass, (up icy mountainous steps) and get to a lake which would get them to the Yukon River. For this they had to build a sturdy boat or float that would pass inspection by the Mounties (police). Sam Steele, the top Mountie, seemed to be a tough lawman but he was trying to save those wretches who would enter this wilderness with inadequate resources. Sam Steele even made the prospective gold miners take a thousand pounds of food! Good he did because some had died by famine. This would also act as a deterrent to the thugs and con men from Skagway and other places from getting into the Yukon. Of course, those criminals were there to try to take things from the law-abiding folks.

As we arrived in Dawson City we were excited of course because this was the center of the greatest gold rush in Alaska/Canada way back in 1897 and going pretty strong until about 1904. During those years an estimated 100 million dollars of gold had been found.

When Skookum Jim (an Indian gold miner) and his group delivered about three thousand pounds of Yukon gold by a ship to Seattle the whole country seemed to be "shookum up" and ready to drop everything and race to the Klondike.

As we looked around Dawson City we could see the vestiges of the former glory days. The quickly built false fronts were still there. The hints of the "Yukon Paris" lingered as the high tastes of oddities and traditional examples were found in the shops.

One of the old grand theaters was there — recently placed back into good repair to remind tourists of the high stepping ladies and the highly acclaimed actors and actresses of the yesteryear. Performances now let visitors enjoy those past venues.

Best of all — for me — was the Keno, a steamboat, anchored now by the government officials so tourists can come to see the last of about 200 plus steamboats that plied the Klondike and Yukon Rivers during that exciting gold rush. It was exciting to take pictures of some of those old steamboats and imagine their skills/actions as they tried to keep afloat when plying the treacherous places of the Yukon River — like the Five Fingers spot — a jutting rock formation appropriately named.

And it was just a good place to visit and relax. Grace and Joanne are approaching with an ice cream cone. They certainly seem to be enjoying that ice cream. It makes me want an ice cream and I hope they still have butter pecan in the store. I would ask Russell to go with me for an ice cream but I saw him tearing off in another direction for whatever. No telling.

Credit: Geri-Gadder Tours of Bainbridge, Ga.; our fellow travelers; KY, IA, MO, SD, WY, MT, Canada, AK info; Whitehorse, Dawson City and Yukon info; personal experiences; personal info; other sources.

We Enjoyed Alaska – But Russell Just About Killed Us!

Mountie keeps law & order at Dawson City

Sam Steele did the same in the Gold Rush

Thanks for Monte Dodge

Like a ghost steamboat it is still there - telling all that Dawson City lured men to gold, glory & death

Part 28
Steamboats, Dredges And Ferries Kept Excitement High

I could not forget those stately old steamboats of the Yukon River and I could not forget those steamers which plied the Ocmulgee River. I was excited. Here were old steamboats preserved in Canada and Alaska and I was able to inspect these vessels. The architecture of these boats (or ships) was impressive and functional. And just like the steamboats of our river (Ocmulgee) a similar type emerged from these vessels.

Like the Mississippi River and the coastal waters the steam craft seemed to first favor the side-wheeler. On the side-wheeler a wheel was placed on each side. With one wheel turning, if desired, great maneuverability was possible. But the one wheel on the back (stern) came to be the popular riverboat because the sternwheeler could squeeze into narrow straits and float and move in shallow waters. With the sternwheeler it was easy to ease up to a dock or landing, like Jacksonville, Ga., and reverse the wheel — making it easy to exit (back out) the landing and continue steaming in the river.

But, in steamboat history it is interesting to note that many of the Ocmulgee River boats were side-wheelers. In fact, the S.M. Manning, a steamboat exploding near Jacksonville, Ga., in 1860, was a side-wheeler. Fourteen passengers were killed and the loud explosion was heard in the town.

But the riverboats busily operated to Dawson City of the Yukon. Over 200 of these steam kickers churned up the waters of the Yukon River and it was tough. After viewing Miles Canyon on the Yukon River I was able to see why many steamboats were uncontrollably "redirected" into turbulent and swift currents or the imposing rock formations.

But we could not stay forever at Dawson City with its great historical archives, artifacts and just plain good stories.

Like the narratives of poet Robert Service, many of these stories were not just fabricated tales. In fact, it is told as truth that one old graveled-voiced gritty gold miner who struck it rich, invested in matrimony. The investment, as it turns out, was one of the saloon's ladies — a pretty entertainer. She was purchased for her weight in pure gold! Nothing was said about her other qualifications. Maybe he got a good deal!

And we enjoyed this place — Dawson City — which had fascinated us with the lore and legends — and some truth — of the old gold rush, the rich strikes, the famine, the churning steamboats, the crusty miners, the durable women, the unscrupulous criminals and the folks who stayed on when others left.

And the folks who stayed deserve at least a notice — the dredgers. Those men operated those huge dredges. To get an idea of what this contraption looked like we will have to show you an image in this book. These mechanical leviathans tore down into the permafrost and heaved up gold not yet uncovered. The machine could do the work of an army of gold miners. Men will always figure out how to get the gold.

Now we face one parting challenge. Putting our bus on that little ferry and putting ourselves on that little ferry. It was the only way to cross the river and Russell and I were not the only ones who doubted that we will be high and dry when, and if, we reach the other bank. Because we remembered what happened at the Jacksonville, Ga., ferry and the Model-T Ford when they attached themselves together and were not compatible. Took a long time for the Model-T to dry out.

Credit: Geri-Gadder Tours of Bainbridge, Ga.; our fellow travelers; KY, IA, MO, SD, WY, MT, Canada, AK info; Whitehorse, Dawson City and Yukon info; personal experiences; personal info; other sources.

Miles Canyon Yukon River Steamboat Obstacles

This Dredge Uncovered Gold When The Old Miners Were Gone

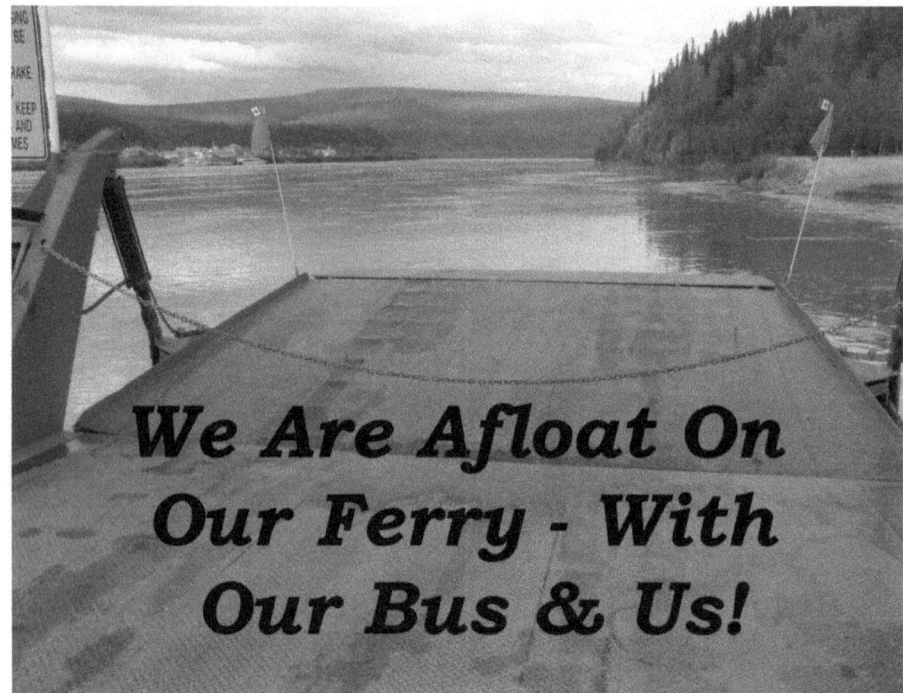

Part 29
Exploding Steamboats Sing A Requiem Of Death

As the Yukon River lightly buffeted our little ferry I delightfully looked for a last time — leaving Canada at Dawson City and heading for Alaska — as I focused on the two steamboats near the town and river. You can see these steamboats because I took a picture so you could see those vessels. And I am glad they are there because those steamboats represent the many steamers that plied those rivers several years back. They were on their way to the Klondike Gold Rush. But my delightful view was tempered with a sadness because I realized the presence of the specter of death that walked the planks and passageways (and boiler!) of those steamboats. Just as it was in the Klondike it was the same with the Ocmulgee River.

So, as I looked on the little "Klondike Spirit," a side-wheeler, I thought about great-great Uncle Joseph Williams being killed on another steamboat side-wheeler, "S.M. Manning." Of course, that was on the Ocmulgee River and near Jacksonville, Ga. That happened in 1860, just before the Civil War, but the memories and memorabilia of that awful disaster still haunt the scene.

Author Mark V. Wetherington in his book, "Plain Folk's Fight," formerly of Milan, Ga., fairly near to Jacksonville, Ga., chronicles "the Bad Death" of that Ocmulgee River steamboat (S.M. Manning) and its passengers.

"The circumstances of their deaths sudden and unexpected, with no chance for family and friends to comfort them in their final moments or hear their dying words - deeply troubled their survivors. Moreover, they died away from home, beyond the family of circle. Indeed, the fact that the men met their end within a few hours' journey of "home, sweet, home" somehow made their deaths all the more difficult to accept and underscored the "uncertainty of life." Not only had these loved ones been unexpectedly snatched from their family circle, but also the violent explosion that "dreadfully scalded" and "horribly mangled" many of their bodies — in some cases, their friends can hardly identify them -

violated the ideal of a Good Death and the sanctity of the corpses. For the family of Telfair County planter Joseph Williams, coming to terms with his death was especially difficult, for his body was lost in the river, whose waters, as one visitor to the scene wrote, 'seem to sing a requiem for the death.'"

And to venture into the Klondike — the gold region — was to open yourself to a "bad death." A few ones found gold and came back to tell about it. But, scores, caught in the infernos of a steamboat, in a ravine or shaft that crumpled, in a train that derailed, in a drunken gunfight or knifing, in shoot-outs with criminals, in fatal envies of a contested romance, a deadly gold claim confrontation or purely from dying — or, starved or overworked or frozen — they were dead.

As we look at those "graveyard steamboats" or the derelicts of old gold dredges or the graves inscribed (and in some cases, no writings) or the creepy sagging buildings we need to honor those lives and their efforts. Their paths paved our roads and made it all possible. We owe them a lot.

And speaking of paths I got a good picture of Russell and Grace going over a swinging bridge on the Yukon River. I was waiting to make sure they made it over before I started crossing over the bridge.

Credit: Geri-Gadder Tours of Bainbridge, Ga.; our fellow travelers; KY, IA, MO, SD, WY, MT, Canada, AK info; Whitehorse, Dawson City and Yukon info; Mark V. Wetherington for a steamboat section on "Plain Folk's Fight"; personal experiences; personal info; other sources.

Waiting to see if the bridge will hold Grace & Russell

The Old Steamboats Claimed Many Lives In Alaska and Georgia

The "S.M. Manning" In 1860 Exploded And Killed Joseph B. Williams And Thirteen More Near Jacksonville, Ga.

Part 30
Unfortunately We Will Always Remember Chicken, Alaska

Russell was excited because we were leaving Canada and the unforgiving tough gold lands of the Yukon. Finally we were now heading for "Beautiful Downtown Chicken, Alaska." Russell had seen about all the Yukon steamboats he wanted to see. He had also seen enough of the ferry. We could not understand why they didn't just build a bridge. (They almost did that but politics got in the way and some folks thought the ferry should stay to lure tourists.) But Russell could agree on Robert Service's poem, "The Land God Forgot":

"O outcast land! O leper land!
Let the lone wolf-cry all express
The hate insensate of thy hand,
Thy heart's abysmal loneliness."

I tried to get Russell to read the poet's Yukon poem about "The Shooting of Dan McGrew" but Russell said he was not interested in reading some Canadian (or Alaskan) "western" that was not really a "western." In fact, it was not even a book — it was a poem!

As we eagerly craned our necks we longed to arrive at "Beautiful Downtown Chicken, Alaska." From the publications we read we just knew this city would be a welcomed oasis of great culture, beautiful scenery, nice restaurants, comfortable lodgings and spectacular entertainment sites. We figured we would never forget Chicken, Alaska.

To begin with, yes, we would never forget Chicken, Alaska. This metropolis had a population of about seventeen people when all were present. But, when they could catch a bush plane they were probably trying to get away from this place!

We were bug-eyed when we surveyed these municipal offerings. There were three buildings — the cafe, the saloon and an emporium (store). The best item in the place was the best-stocked inventory of unlimited postcards! Not to mention an $18.95 T-shirt and some odd novelties.

We were entertained by sticking our heads into multicolored plywood "chicken" forms. Everything there revolved around "chickens." The town was supposed to be named "Ptarmigan," the Alaska state fowl. (The "p," like pneumonia, is silent.) But the "fowl" folded when the citizens cried "foul" because they could not spell or say "ptarmigan." Some were spelling/saying "Tarmigan" — some were using "Carmagan" — some "Termigen" — and some other creative spellings and sayings. But Alaskan folks are indeed creative. They are also realistic and practical. So they named the town "Chicken" because, and truly, it resembled a ptarmigan. Now they could say and spell "chicken." Problem solved. That bird called a ptarmigan could just stay etched on the great Alaska state emblem that signifies the state fowl.

Interestingly we found that Chicken, Alaska, shuts down the road during the winter. Mail comes in by plane (weather permitting) on Tuesdays and Fridays. No cell phones. No telephones. If you go up the road and hold your head just right you might get a cell phone signal. School operates by correspondence.

And, the outhouse behind the gift shop operates without the aid of civilized plumbing. We won't reveal the name of that building but it is certainly named with a graphic label! Connected to "chicken."

Russell, just gave me a bad look and shook his head. "Chicken" was quickly becoming Russell's whole image, epitome and embodiment of the whole country of Alaska. He hated the whole place but he could not find it in his heart to refuse getting five postcards to remember this unforgettable location. And a quick trip to the outhouse and we were out of Chicken. Hopefully, permanently.

Credit: Geri-Gadder Tours of Bainbridge, Ga.; our fellow travelers; KY, IA, MO, SD, WY, MT, Canada, AK info; Dawson City and Chicken, AK info; personal experiences; personal info; other sources.

Grace   Russell

Welcome to "Beautiful Downtown CHICKEN, Alaska"!

Part 31
Sometimes The Absence Dominates The Presence

Russell was not excited for the next Alaskan experiences because he was wearily being worn thin with all the hugeness of this whole excursion. He could not understand why this "great place" had not advanced to at least a modicum of civilization. He might not have used that exact terminology but it means the same thing. I tried to tell him that Alaska was not made a state until 1959; but he was resolute. He said they had plenty of time to get their act together and the sooner he left this forsaken place the better he would like it.

Along this route was no place to change Russell's opinion. Over this road, sometimes very bumpy, there was a definite scarcity of adequate restrooms. Contrary to that, the restrooms were primitive looking outhouses that appeared to hang over the deep cliffs. I would not want to get near the rear of one of those outhouses.

The men made it pretty good but there were many more women and they had to wait in long lines for the one outhouse. It was not easy or comfortable and some had to seek refuge in the back of the bus restroom. I don't know what we would have done without that facility.

One lady traveler seemed to be determined to make things go as they should. In other words she expected fellow travelers to be punctilious and brief when it came to staying in the restroom (or outhouse). One time a little lady traveler took just a little more time in the outhouse than this lady thought necessary. After quite a spell in the outhouse, this lady exclaimed, "Well, well, perhaps she is knitting a sweater in there." So, I think the patience of the folks started wearing thin in this excursion. But it was still fun and the varieties of events made it worthwhile.

For instance, although we did not catch or see a single living wild salmon, that I know of, another Newnan traveler with another trip, sent me a fine picture of a bear and his two cubs enjoying a lunch of salmon.

All the types of salmon — chinook, king, pink and all the other types fascinated me and I was intrigued with the life cycle which brought those fish from the freshwater to the sea and brought them right back to their freshwater native place from whence they came. If you caught one of those king salmon I bet you had about all you could bring in! How about a 40-pounder!

Then, to Russell's great expectation, we were now heading for the great outdoors to see many birds and animals. According to the knowledgeable guides and park rangers we would probably see more animals than we could stir with a stick. I must put you on notice — the operational word in this last sentence is "probably." We saw very few species of wildlife. This was after boarding the bus at 6 AM and riding for hours. Our assigned antediluvian rejected school bus creakily negotiated narrow dirt roads and hairpin curves. If you slipped off the road you had about 700 feet plus before hitting the bottom!

I will show you the poor old moose who did not have the stamina to move — much less exhibit any spirited motion (as wheeling, darting or running). Russell looked over his glasses and said, "What a pitiful creature." About the same time, Russell and I concluded that some park ranger must have tied him to a sapling so we could see this "wildlife." We also came to the conclusion that they did not have to "tie" the animal. He probably would have stayed right there because he did not look like he had the energy to seek a relocation.

You see some strange things in Alaska. Sometimes you see things and sometimes you do not see things. And I was determined to see at least one animal on this great Talkeetna adventure (not counting the lame moose). I saw a bird and chased him until I could get him out in the road. I took his picture. I don't think you even want to see that bird.

Credit: Geri-Gadder Tours of Bainbridge, Ga.; our fellow travelers; KY, IA, MO, SD, WY, MT, Canada, AK info; Talkeetna, AK info; personal experiences; personal info; other sources.

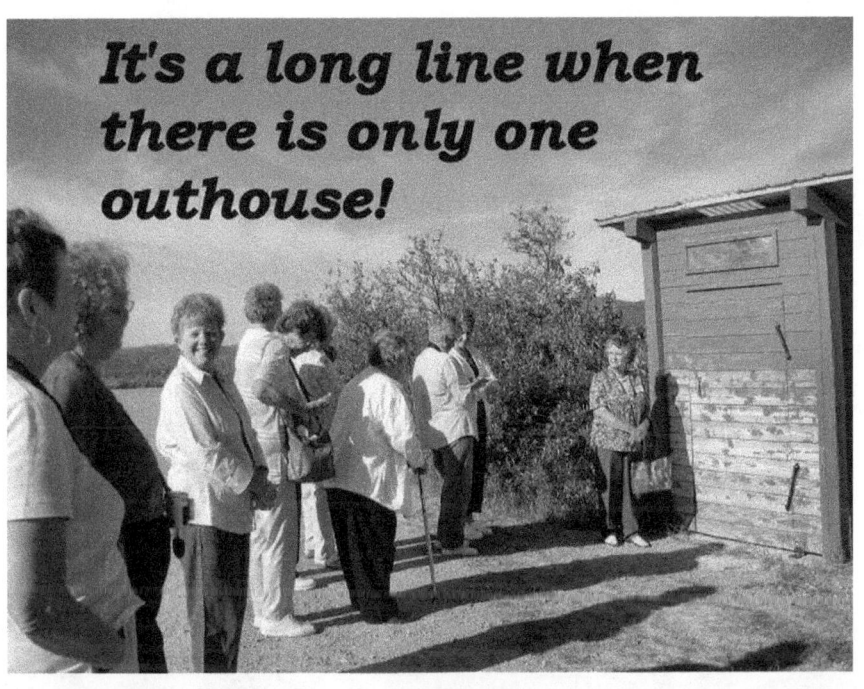

It's a long line when there is only one outhouse!

Russell said this moose was a "pitiful creature."

We thought someone tied the moose to a sapling so tourists could see "wildlife."

Credit: Steve Keeble, fellow Alaskan traveler

Part 32
The Great Moose Dropping Festival
– And We Missed It

But we were not through with the events and the non-events of Talkeetna. This place is somewhere between Anchorage and Fairbanks and these folks, like other Alaskans, can come up with some pretty creative doings. But we are good at either getting to these great events too early or too late. Alas, we were going to miss the Moose Dropping Festival!

We just missed the great Moose Dropping Festival occurring at Talkeetna. By only a couple of days. But just hearing of this event would get the curiosity up of the most detached and indifferent tourists.

We included a little cartoon about the Moose Dropping but it does not exactly happen like that. Here is the straight information on carrying out the Moose Drop. A moose is not hoisted to a helicopter or tower. However, a product of the moose is pulled up to a great height. This product is a manageable handful "patty" of moose manure. Many patties. The dried manure bit, probably about the size of an egg, is now treated with several coats of shellac. This makes it hard enough to keep it together — this little clump — and keep it separated from the others. This little tough exterior chunk, with the others, is now ready for the next step. This involves placing a number on each "moose drop clump" (thoroughly hardened by the shellac). When thousands are numbered you have what amounts to a lottery.

Now, the numbered pieces are placed in a huge net and pulled upward to a high tower or hoisted on a helicopter. The object is to get that net, with all the "manure eggs," to a great height. After this is accomplished, citizens gather at the ground area and surround a great target which is painted on the ground.

The next object is to turn all those flying manure bits off into the blue yonder and let them have its way with gravity. Anxiously the citizens watch the missiles - hoping that the manure bits, with their own number(s), hit the center of the target. Owing to the tough but forgiving

Alaskan personalities they not only award a prize to the closest to the bulls-eye. They also award a prize who finds his wayward moose pellet the farthest. I think it is magnanimous and kind that they try to address the fortunate and the unfortunate. Not every day do you hit or miss a moose poop missile.

At this point I did not know what to do about Russell because I would feel like he would want to go back to the Moose Drop. Like I said you would probably only get one swing (or catch) at this chance.

Also, in great mixed emotions, I know, and Russell knew, of another great adventure looming on the horizon. It was, probably a one-time shot, like the Moose Drop. This other event was none other than being able to ride in a snowmobile in a glacier. Plodding through the ice fields we would get inside the snowmobile and take off for the glacier. We thought they needed to pump a little air in those tires but they informed us that the tires had to be flat to negotiate the glacier. We had doubts of it being able to run fast, if necessary.

But we missed the snowmobile. Unfortunate.

Unfortunately, again, we did not get to play the moose drop or put our numbers on one of those envied nuggets. Other favored ones would have to take our places and gain entry with their chips and whatever those moose muffins brought. It was a bitter pill but we would adjust and head northward.

That great mountain was out there — Denali, once called Mount McKinley. The great pinnacle is 20,320 ft. and it is the king of the hill. We looked forward to be able to view this majestic mountain.

You guessed it. Clouds came over and we had to look for a substitute. We did not see Denali and we never saw it. Like I said, some things you see in Alaska and sometimes you do not see things. But I would certainly have liked to see the Great Moose Dropping Festival. Russell and I will just have to try to get back up there. Alaska! You never know!

Credit: Geri-Gadder Tours of Bainbridge, Ga.; our fellow travelers; KY, IA, MO, SD, WY, MT, Canada, AK info; Talkeetna, AK info; personal experiences; personal info; other sources.

Russell could not decide between a Snowmobile Tour and The Moose Dropping Festival – tough call.

Part 33
Moose Droppings, Bingo And A Bearded Man

I suppose all of us were surprised, or taken back, that an Alaska festival would create a happy time around the idea of dropping moose dried excrement pieces from the sky, hoping the pieces would land on a target. After the free-fall hunks landed, some lucky person on the bulls-eye would receive a gift from a random (numbered) moose pellet.

The great moose BM scattered dispensation was almost as brilliant as the folks from Jacksonville, Georgia, who were credited with creating the popular game Bingo (originally called Beano). A toy salesman came through Jacksonville, Ga., in 1929, liked it, took the Beano game to New York and changed the name to Bingo. Surely, someone up in Alaska will also think of a catchy name for the moose dropping affair and it will probably challenge and maybe surpass Bingo. I know some of you are already trying to come up with a winner.

Following this mental exercise, timely and appropriately, Russell spent some time wondering about missing The Great Alaskan Moose Dropping. It would be interesting to see the festival. Was it a challenging and interesting game? Someone from South Carolina had suggested that participants might even throw the moose pieces like a discus — if the moose pieces were shaped like dried cow patties (or buffalo patties). Truly, many calls are coming in from other states to ask about the moose festival. I look for more calls and emails.

But Russell did not dwell long on the possibility of throwing dried moose excrement chunks. The potentiality was still present — picking up a memento that had manifested a freshly dropped odoriferous pile — certainly causing distinct stinking negative results. With that thought Russell abandoned the whole theme and any conceptualization of a Moose Dropping event. Instead, Russell looked forward to see what was coming around the Talkeetna wilderness trail curve (providing the old bus could stay in the road and not run over a cliff).

Russell, more quickly than he thought, was about to experience his highlight of the tour. Abruptly, the old bus squealed to a halt and out of the bushes emerged an outdoorsman par excellence. From a distance he appeared to have great experience about the hinterlands — a hardy expert enriching and exhilarating any tourist who breathed his words. Russell could not wait to land right next to his seat. He would hear of great adventure! This young man must have camped, fished, hunted, and faced the horrors of big bears, snakes and other fierce wildlife. Russell got close to this man so he would not miss any information.

The bearded man must have done all that stuff plus other things and evidently he must have been real busy with all that. What he had not been able to facilitate for about a month and a half was to take a bath. Lice could not have penetrated his locks because his hair was matted as hard as those shellac-hardened moose missiles. Russell never got to breathe his words much because he was breathing the great physical aura emanating from this man. His more than tinged air/atmosphere really was mellow — way past mellow. I believe he would have made the Goat Man hold his nose!

As soon as Russell got his breath he careened, pale as a sheet, back to his own seat and Grace grabbed her nose. Russell started looking for an airplane immediately — anywhere — hoping to be rescued by a local bush plane pilot. Back to Georgia. He had seen and smelled about all he wanted up here in Alaska!

Russell swore that the buffaloes we saw out on the road were mild compared to this wilderness fellow. But we benefited because the haggard man told us how to scare off the bears. He said just stand as tall as you can and make menacing sounds toward the bear. But, to tell you the truth, I think the smell got to the bears!

Credit: Geri-Gadder Tours of Bainbridge, Ga.; our fellow travelers; KY, IA, MO, SD, WY, MT, Canada, AK info; Talkeetna, AK info; personal experiences; personal info; other sources.

Russell Was Wanting To Kick Out The Emergency Window!

Russell wanted to get this pilot to take him to Georgia. He had had enough!

These buffaloes were good-smelling creatures compared to our outdoorsman visitor.

Part 34
Big Steamboat, Iditarod Trainers And Our Visit To Chena Village

As I read the newspaper recently I noticed a press clip telling about the *USS ALASKA* coming to Kings Bay, Georgia. Thinking about the super submarine made me think again of Alaska. It also made me think of our travel to Alaska. It made me remember the bigness, the uniqueness and the importance of that state. In fact, it is almost so unique, so located logistically and strategically, that I almost want to call it a country — a separate nation.

Traveling to Fairbanks, Alaska, renews that trip as we stopped at Chena Village and looked around Steamboat Landing. They told us we would be getting on a steamboat but I never thought it would be such a steamboat! The paddle kicker was tremendous! The Discovery III was a sight to see. Someone took Joanne and me (picture) with the vessel in our background.

In the brochure we found that a family built a steamboat way back in 1868 and they progressively built bigger and better steamboats. The last one, Discovery III, which we rode up the Chena River, is 156 ft. long, carries 900 passengers and has 4 decks. As I said, you can see it is a large boat.

But the best part was not the ride up the river. In addition to seeing some unusual dwellings and scenery we were treated to a great event.

The captain stopped so we could see what was going on at the bank. Nearby dog trainers were working with sled dogs. And not just any dogs, either. They were training the dogs that would run in the Iditarod Race. I think someone said the race from Anchorage to Nome was more than 1,000 miles.

Not only were we witnessing the place of this training but we were on the site of probably the most famous winner of the Iditarod Race - Susan Butcher. Unfortunately, Susan died in 2006 of leukemia but she had won four races in the Iditarod. But her work continued.

And the slogan of the Alaska submarine fit the slogan of Alaskans, including Susan Butcher — alert, confident, able. With this slogan Alaskans have caused them to be a great country. Made of great people.

By the way, you are looking at a picture which depicts one routine of dog sledding practice. One of the trainers told us that the dogs would pull the ATV (four-wheeler) very fast and he had to stay on the brake to keep the dogs from going too fast. Dog training is very rigorous and the tactics are always debated — some folks think they are doing it right and the other folks think the dogs are being abused.

But, in 1925, some mighty able dogs and some effective mushers brought sled dogging to front page headlines. Racing to beat time, these dogs and mushers, in relay, delivered a serum that saved hundreds of people. The Iditarod Race still represents that spirit.

Moving from the spirited dogs we steamed to the Chena Indian Village. Here the Athabascan Indians were fascinating. They told how they prepared the furs of the bears, moose, caribou and other animals. And told us about their history and culture.

In another picture you see a young Indian maiden modeling one of the beautiful parka outfits. If I remember correctly she said this particular coat sold for $3,000. You might think they think a lot of their coats but if you could see one you would agree that the workmanship was superb. But, it seems that they have moved past our limit. Anyway, I didn't see any of our travelers leaving with one of those furs! We would have to look for other trinkets.

Alaska — history, pride, diverse people, financial resources in gold, salmon, furs, pipelines of oil and gas, creative efforts to achieve the summit of a hard environment. These people have a right to be proud — Alaska.

Credit: Geri-Gadder Tours of Bainbridge, Ga.; our fellow travelers; KY, IA, MO, SD, WY, MT, Canada, AK info; Fairbanks, AK info; personal experiences; personal info; other sources.

This steamboat was a little bigger than the one at Old Jacksonville, Ga.

This trainer had to hold down the brake to control the dogs!

Part 35
Fairbanks Was Great But Russell Was 4,439 Miles From Douglas, Georgia

We were in a nice place — Fairbanks, Alaska. But to look at Russell I could tell he was not happy. He had his trusty map out again and was figuring the distance from Fairbanks, AK, to Douglas, GA. When Russell adjusts his eyeglasses to a knowing angle and picks up his ever-present pencil he becomes a dangerous man. When he clears his throat he becomes even more dangerous. At this serious juncture he continued with his calculations and had just about written on and rubbed on his map so much it looked like the paper was part of the old Dead Sea scrolls. Nonetheless, Russell tapped his map, whatever was left of it, grimaced and said, "I thought we were heading for home — do you know how far we have to go — 4,439 miles!"

This revealing new dimension of our country (the USA), now etched on Russell's brain, had converted "a right good ways" to the staggering numerical equivalence of 4,439 miles. As I looked at Russell he got that starry look and appeared to be looking for an airplane. I was a little concerned because I again thought that Russell might try to catch a plane and leave us.

Pretty soon we feared this conclusion was correct because we could not find Russell anywhere. In this picture of Joanne, Grace and me, you can readily see that Russell is not in the photo. He was gone. We would have to look for him immediately.

At this location we had motored (in our bus) to a part of the Alaska University known as the Georgeson Botanical Gardens. But it was a huge place. If Russell had not absconded with one of the planes nearby but rather had behaved himself at all, we figured, with good luck, we would find him in the gardens.

My first thought was that Russell might be in the section of the big cabbages. Two reasons — Russell had been impressed with the big cabbages we marveled over at the Chena Indian Village. Next, Russell likes cabbage — especially if it is cooked with some bacon. And that is just where we found him — admiring those huge cabbages. You can see from the picture that you could eat a long time with one of those cabbages. But we figured that Haskell White, our tour director, would frown at taking one of those cabbages on the bus. Also, with Russell's previous luck, one of those Canadian border police would probably just confiscate his cabbage. It was hard to get ahead in this Alaska-Canada borderline crisscross.

An effort to get Russell off some of this negative thinking resulted in trying to get him interested in the "Alaska's Unknown Family." This is a central statue at Fairbanks, AK, and spotlights the history, heritage, cultural and other things of past, present and future ideals of this great state. The photo is shown here.

Russell was not interested in the statue. He muttered something to the effect that if that family was unknown and they didn't even know who they were themselves how in the tarnation did they think that he would know who they were!

I could very well see that things were not going good for Russell. He had enjoyed very little of this town, with the exception of the cabbages, and I was not about to mention one of the outstanding July events in Fairbanks.

It was the contest of the bearded men with the hairy chests and hairy legs. It was the epitome of the macho Alaska man. Somehow, I could not bring myself to suggest this attraction to Russell. He had suffered enough being cooped up with the stinking wilderness man on the wildlife tour bus.

In fact, I was about like Russell. I started tracing my map. Also I noticed it was wearing a little thin too. From what I can tell we will be finally heading for south when we leave Fairbanks. It is 4,439 miles but it is at least headed in the right direction — South!

Credit: Geri-Gadder Tours of Bainbridge, Ga.; our fellow travelers; KY, IA, MO, SD, WY, MT, Canada, AK info; Fairbanks, AK info; personal experiences; personal info; other sources.

We Enjoyed Alaska – But Russell Just About Killed Us!

It seems that Russell has gotten away. We cannot find him anywhere.

Grace　Joanne　Julian

Russell liked these cabbages – reminded him of Georgia!

Part 36
North Pole And Santa And Wife Posed With Us For A Picture

I absolutely refused to believe that we were on our way to the North Pole — and Santa Claus! All the folks on the bus were talking about the reindeer, Santa Claus and the Santa Claus House. After awhile someone hollered, "There is the North Pole!" I was back in the bus and I could not see this great sight and still would not believe this magical place with St. Nick, flying reindeer and small elves — all working hard exceeding boys' and girls' expectations of bountiful gifts and goodies for Christmas.

And were we lucky! Believe it or not — standing right here with us — Santa Claus and Mrs. Santa Claus! We met them and I expected their hands to be very cold but we were here in July so their hands were about average. However, their hands had been cold before. We were told the weather was so unpredictable that one summer got to 95 degrees (very warm) and a cold winter night the frigid weather reached -78 (yes, MINUS 78) degrees. It would have frozen Russell to a long icicle. Russell just shivered at the thought of being stranded up there in the freezing winter. Needless to say, Russell looked up toward the sky and you could just imagine what he was thinking — a plane headed for the South!

However, Mr. and Mrs. Claus were very nice and even agreed to pose with us in a picture. They were very busy in the shop and I didn't think they would do that but as you can see (from the picture with this article) we are together in the picture.

The reindeer I inspected back of the shop did not impress me but I think they were molting (shedding their hair). Surely they will be back in great shape as they blast off the North Pole launch pad and head for the skies as they help Santa distribute all those packages.

You can see another picture here that tells about the elves. They were working so hard I think they had those at another shop because we could hear a lot of noise out there — sawing, hammering and the like.

But we could see a lot of stuff they had made because there were many things in the North Pole gift shop. Unfortunately, those items did not get on the sleigh, go down the chimney and wound up at our Christmas tree. If you got one of those gifts here at the shop you had to produce Mastercard, cash or something equivalent. I think they even took that funny money from Canada. And horrors, the mention of that, we would be heading back to Canada soon.

Also, never think the North Pole had all nice people — some were naughty! A picture shows what they do with naughty people. This police car was ready to dispatch and rein anyone trying to get rowdy. Of course, our friend J.L. Sutton, was not being naughty but he wanted to get a picture of this cruiser. I think he had it taken so he could tell Russell that he had better straighten up because these officers might be as tough as the border police and the Canadian Mounties waiting at the border. It was our belief that the Mounties would capture Russell again but he was practicing being real little in hopes that the officers would not notice him this next time.

But it was time to leave the North Pole, Alaska, and it was fun. But, I still have hope that Russell will adapt and adopt the culture of this great state of Alaska. I am not sure but I think I saw him talking to a policeman near his car — about his tires. About coming back in the winter. Wanted to know whether to use studs or chains for his car.

There is always a chance that Russell will welcome this great land with open arms. But it is only a sliver of hope, so very slight, that he will bend to that wonderful persuasion. So, be that way, Russell, we are heading for Canada. You had better get real little!

Credit: Geri-Gadder Tours of Bainbridge, Ga.; our fellow travelers; KY, IA, MO, SD, WY, MT, Canada, AK info; North Pole, AK info; personal experiences; personal info; other sources.

We Enjoyed Alaska – But Russell Just About Killed Us!

Part 37
Alaska's Boney Courthouse
Connected To Telfair County, Georgia

Before we leave Alaska I need to return to the city of Anchorage. To Boney Courthouse. Boney Courthouse is important to me because it is a part of my heritage and a place, including all of Alaska, where one of our relatives "staked down a claim." Not a claim formed and approved to mine gold but the kind of gold that translated into hard work, a brilliant mind, sagacity, creative ideas, correct judicial behavior, pioneering new legal horizons and a gem of one of the renowned giants of Alaska's bursting new state. He was a driven man dedicated to driven purposes. His name was Chief Justice George F. Boney of the Alaska Supreme Court. Boney Courthouse bears his name.

About the only way I can claim Mr. Boney is because our Williams ancestors came from North Carolina with the Boney ancestors way back in 1823 to China Hill near Old Jacksonville, Georgia. And the Williamses and the Boneys married and their branches grew and produced many generations and progeny. Oh, another reason I claim all the Boneys — they invite me from time to time to come to the annual Boney Reunion at China Hill near Old Jacksonville. But the dichotomy of mine at the Ocmulgee River and Mr. Boney's domain in Alaska got separated quite a bit - in geography and effective production. But that does not keep me from admiring a fellow who made quite a mark, even though that life was cut short at the age of 42. Justice Boney died in 1972 in a boating accident.

I never got to talk with Justice Boney. But I talked with his brother recently — Tom Boney. I quickly found that this world is a small one. Tom Boney played football at South Georgia College for Coach Bobby Bowden. Tom Boney plans to attend the reunion when the Bowden fellowship again gathers in Douglas, Ga., the last weekend of May. Between the SGC playing time, Tom also played at the University of Tampa and Presbyterian.

I could tell that Tom Boney liked people, progress and His God (and That Providence guides all). Even though I had never met him I could tell from his enthusiasm, his memories, his past endeavors, his present situation, his future plans — that he was a good one. Not only that, I picked up immediately that he loved to tell of the credits and plaudits of other friends. I could see quickly how Tom fit the character and countenance of the Boneys. Without a doubt he was one of those.

I asked Tom how their parents got to Jacksonville, Florida, from Jacksonville, Georgia, (or China Hill). Tom said the working situation moved them to Savannah, Ga. This is where George F. Boney was born. In a little while the parents returned to China Hill and George F. Boney attended elementary school at China Hill. Later the family moved to Jacksonville, Florida.

Those schoolmasters at China Hill probably did not realize the caliber of prodigy in the midst of their humble classroom. We never know how some will turn out. We need to encourage and teach each child. One, or more, might do great things. And, as Grandmother Anderson said, if they don't "behave in a great way", they can certainly "just behave." I told Tom Boney we might be related in another way. Her mother was an Anderson before marrying the Mr. Boney, Sr. My maternal side is Anderson. You never know.

Chief Justice George F. Boney had a lot of ties to China Hill near Jacksonville, Ga. And in another article we will tell you some more about George Boney. And some more about these Boneys. They are an interesting family.

Credit: Geri-Gadder Tours of Bainbridge, Ga.; our fellow travelers; KY, IA, MO, SD, WY, MT, Canada, AK info; Anchorage, AK; Boney Courthouse; info on Tom Boney; personal experiences; personal info; other sources.

BONEY COURTHOUSE
Anchorage, Alaska

Named For
Chief Justice George F. Boney
Of The Supreme Court of Alaska

Anchorage, Alaska's Largest City, Is Bustling With People And Beauty

Part 38
Chief Justice Boney Was Close To China Hill, Near Jacksonville, Georgia

Well, we are back to resume our article about Chief Justice George Boney. Just standing there at Boney Courthouse in Anchorage, Alaska, made me wonder how in the world did Mr. Boney wind up in Alaska! From what I learned from Tom Boney, a brother, Mr. Boney got there via the military. George Boney served as a judge advocate (lawyer) in the military service and his travels guided him to that enchanted land.

I don't think I am far from the truth — that Mr. Boney and Alaska were made for each other. The adventure, the risk taking, the work, his ability and blending with the multi-ethnic fabric of this great land just suited Mr. Boney. Here he was able to help form a new state and give direction to uncharted territory. He was in his bailiwick. He was on his turf.

To begin to understand George Boney we can go way back to his high school when he was 15 years of age. He and two buddies at Andrew Jackson High School at Jacksonville, FL, came to China Hill, Ga., near Jacksonville, Ga., and led a revival at Bethel Methodist Church. Young George was doing some of the preaching. This was a pilgrimage to George Boney because this place was the home of the Boneys. The connection of this place meant something to George Boney. Another indicator that tells us how much it meant to him was the fact that he maintained his Masonic lodge membership at the General John Coffee Chapter at Bethel Methodist Church (upper room) at China Hill, Ga.

George Boney's running the Bethel Methodist Church revival with his buddies also tells us something about this young man who would become the youngest Chief Justice of a Supreme Court of a state in the nation up to that time. These buddies were also high octane performers. One boy was named Pettigrew and the other was Sessums. They would also make their marks. Later, Richard A. Pettigrew became the House Speaker and Senator of the State of Florida. His work would take a volume. The other boy, T. Terrell Sessums became the president of the student body at the University of Florida. Later he became the Speaker of the House and was Chairman of the Florida Regents (Universities) and was honored by a school with his name. But back in the 1940s they were holding a revival in the Bethel Methodist Church at China Hill, Ga. They had the faith.

The Boneys are pretty good in keeping in touch with each others. They still have those old-fashioned reunions (at Bethel Church at China Hill) and if you look up on the hill at China Hill you will see a historical marker telling about the Boneys. I will include this marker so you can see it.

Also, I will do a little chart that will show the lineage of the Boneys (and the branching of the lineage that includes Chief Justice Boney of Alaska).

Especially I like the epitaph of the old ancestor, Cullen Boney, as it goes like this:

"Behold ye strangers passing by
as you are now so once was I.
As I am now so you must be.
Prepare for death and follow me."

I look forward to seeing Tom Boney and Howell Boney in the near future. They are going to the Bobby Bowden reunion but they are also returning to worship services at the old church — Bethel Methodist Church at China Hill, Ga.

It is good to see folks returning to their roots and the old places of their ancestors. It also tells you a lot about folks. Much like cement, like the cement (no weeds) covering the ground of the entire Boney Cemetery at China Hill, Ga. A hard foundation for living here — and a permanent resting place for physical death and the glory of spiritual eternity. A durable faith.

Credit: Geri-Gadder Tours of Bainbridge, Ga.; our fellow travelers; KY, IA, MO, SD, WY, MT, Canada, AK info; Anchorage, AK; Tom Boney info on Justice George Boney; Telfair County History; personal info; other sources.

We Enjoyed Alaska – But Russell Just About Killed Us! 147

Three Young Men In High School Brought A Revival To China Hill, Ga. To Bethel Meth. Church

Later In Life The Three Men Continued Their Excellent Leadership

George Boney, Chief Justice, Alaska

Richard Pettigrew, Florida House of Speaker, Senator

Terrell Sessums, Speaker of House, Fla.

This Marker Stands At China Hill, Ga. Near Old Jacksonville.

This Family Came To Telfair County From North Carolina With The Williams Family In 1823.

Alexander Boney
(1863 - 1946)
Grandfather of

Chief Justice
George F. Boney
of
The Alaska Supreme Court

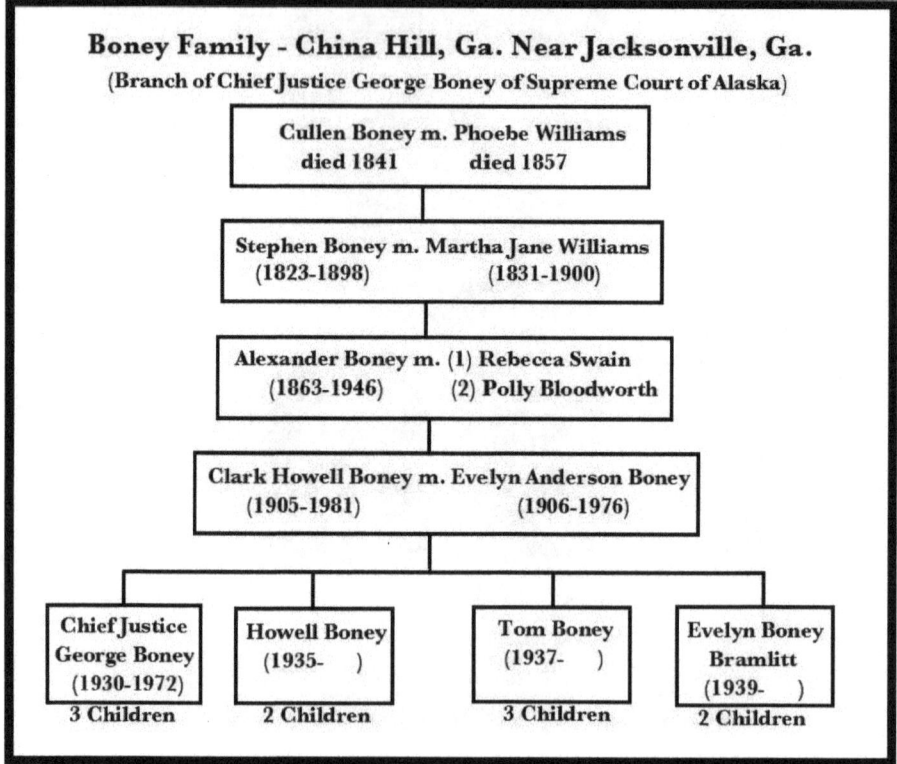

Part 39
Chief Justice Boney's History Welded With His Humanity

Metal-detecting. I thought about Chief Justice George Boney when I was up there at China Hill, Ga., a few days ago. I was up there with Cash McCall and we were metal-detecting. It really brings in another dimension of history. We certainly appreciate Frank Lee and Sonny Royal and others who let us look around Jacksonville, Ga., and China Hill, Ga.

And, I don't know, but I bet Justice George Boney would have loved metal-detecting. I say that because his actions reflect a natural ability to ferret out the missing jig-saw pieces of the court process. And it didn't take him long to decide to do something about the missing items — like Davy Crockett — "Be always sure you are right — then go ahead." Because of this proclivity toward common sense organization and a tireless work ethic Justice Boney soon set the wheels going and better things were happening. Some even called him "The Innovator."

Evidently, Justice Boney remembered his history and traditions from China Hill because this trait was still strong as he moved the justice process along in Alaska. I like what one man from Alaska said about Justice Boney:

"Of special significance to me, as president of the Anchorage Bar, was the way Chief Justice Boney tended the relationship between Bench and Bar. He recognized that a warm, frank and enlightened relationship would not only improve the day-to-day function of the judicial system, but would affect it in years to come in a manner significant to the bench, to the Bar, and to the public we serve. In this regard, as in others, the Chief Justice possessed that keen sense of history commensurate with his high office." (Remarks of R. Everett Harris, President of Anchorage Bar Association)

This "sense of history" was welded with his "sense of humanity." In fact, Mr. Boney revealed his philosophy and belief when he said,

"The law has to fit humanity."

And that was not just idle fancy talk. The man walked in these paths and worked to achieve that ideal.

Even earlier when Justice Boney was young he tried to get young people involved in church. He would go out and recruit youngsters to come to church and be active in church activities. Some of the Alaskans even said, with his zeal, that Justice Boney, had he followed the clergy route he "would have given the Rev. Billy Graham stiff competition."

Recalling young George Boney and his buddies doing a revival at the age of 15 also reminds me that I need to include a picture of the old Bethel Methodist Church. The old church was the one George preached at during the revival. The old church was toppled by a tornado in 1957. Big oak trees were flipped over like they were coffee weeds.

When I thought about George missing the China Hill tornado in 1957 I thought about the 1964 earthquake he was in Alaska. Valdez, near Anchorage, was flattened and destroyed. Some 133 died. That was a bad time for Alaska. They have a lot of volcano and earthquake activity.

But Chief Justice George Boney measured the events of those calamities as he measured the events of his own success. He always tried to make "humanity" a large part of the process. He knew high and tall towers reach to the skies but he knew well that those could come crushing down — like the firetower at China Hill, Ga. And like old Bethel Church. You have to watch fires and tornadoes.

Mr. Boney even had a favorite about fires (and other items):

"We should never burn down the barn of constitutional liberties to get one rat." There were other ways to catch the rat.

That says a lot about "The Chief," history, humanity, common sense, restraint, righteousness and patience. Chief Justice Boney left us some rich stuff.

Credit: Geri-Gadder Tours of Bainbridge, Ga.; our fellow travelers; KY, IA, MO, SD, WY, MT, Canada, AK info; Anchorage, AK; Tom Boney info on Justice George Boney; Telfair County History; R. Everett Harris, President, Anchorage Bar Association; Sonny Royal; Frank Lee; personal info; other sources.

We Enjoyed Alaska – But Russell Just About Killed Us!

And, I don't know, but I bet Justice George Boney would have loved metal-detecting.

Tornado Blew Down China Hill Firetower

Bethel United Methodist Church, China Hill, GA. Destroyed by tornado in 1957.

Part 40
Harvard Law School Was Not Ready For George Boney

Southern traditions, like Alaskan traditions, seem to have a way of hanging around. At least the better traditions - the ones that are honorable and lasting. Like courage, and hospitality and fair-mindedness. And shunning bad practices — pretentiousness and shallow thinking and back-knifing social climbing. George Boney was raised up to reach for the best traditions.

Nevertheless, against the tide, George Boney wound up at Harvard at the law school. Obviously he was amongst a lot of folks who did not act like George — in fact, they didn't even understand George Boney.

Laughing later, Derek Bok, later President of Harvard who was a classmate of George Boney, tells us a few things about George. The Harvard student body was just not ready for George Boney.

President Bok said, *"He said that, in his day, at least, the Harvard Law School was a fairly sophisticated place and tended to be populated with people from the North and from the Eastern Seaboard. If you had a Southern accent, you were considered presumptively ignorant. As we all know, George was endowed with both a keen and very broad mind, and he had many great attributes which we have all known in our encounters with him. But he had to endure the putdown of having a Southern accent."*

Bok, also the Dean of the Law School, before becoming President of Harvard, continued, *"George, throughout his life, seemed by chance to make friends with people who later occupied significant positions in the world. He was warm, lighthearted, he had a jolly attitude and a sense of humor in an atmosphere where most people were quite tense and preoccupied with the furtherance of their own careers."* Someone said this quite aptly describes the atmosphere at an institution like Harvard Law School.

But, it appears that seeing is believing, for George's classmates, as they discovered quickly, he was a brilliant person, a tenacious student and a likable and engaging colleague. Not only they discovered that George had graduated with great honors at the University of Georgia with his bachelor's degree but he was repeating a like performance at the Harvard Law School as he gleaned high marks and was the coveted recipient of the Roscoe Pound Prize. That one does not come in a Cracker Jack box.

But George had the work-ethic down pretty well. Earlier, in his neighborhood he got up early before school and distributed a newspaper in the area. With his brothers George worked hard at manual tasks and put away money for their schooling. One of these jobs took George to sea where he was a waiter on a merchant ship in the merchant marine.

But, evidently George was not just a cookie cutter craftsman. He tried new things. He was not afraid of risk. And trying creative maneuvers. One judge recalled one of George's efforts. At an earlier time, George was in a law practice in Alaska. If he won or lost, he tried to do his best for his client. After losing an effort at the Supreme Court of Alaska George Boney caught a plane and went to Washington, D.C., and caught United States Supreme Court Justice Hugo Black at home. He was able to talk to him and get a stay of execution on the Supreme Court decision. George was the first to try that. He was a hard worker.

A fellow attorney once said, *"(We will) always remember him as a first class lawyer and judge, a first class citizen, and a first class human being."*

One man laughed and said George had to borrow his Buick when Mr. Boney had to host other judges at a meeting. They couldn't get into his car. He had a Camaro. Even a few around China Hill and Jacksonville, Ga., tried that model. It was cutting-edge — like George.

Credit: Geri-Gadder Tours of Bainbridge, Ga.; our fellow travelers; KY, IA, MO, SD, WY, MT, Canada, AK info; Anchorage, AK; Tom Boney info on Justice George Boney; Attorney Donald A. Burr; Justice Roger G. Connor; President of Harvard, Derek Bok; personal info; other sources.

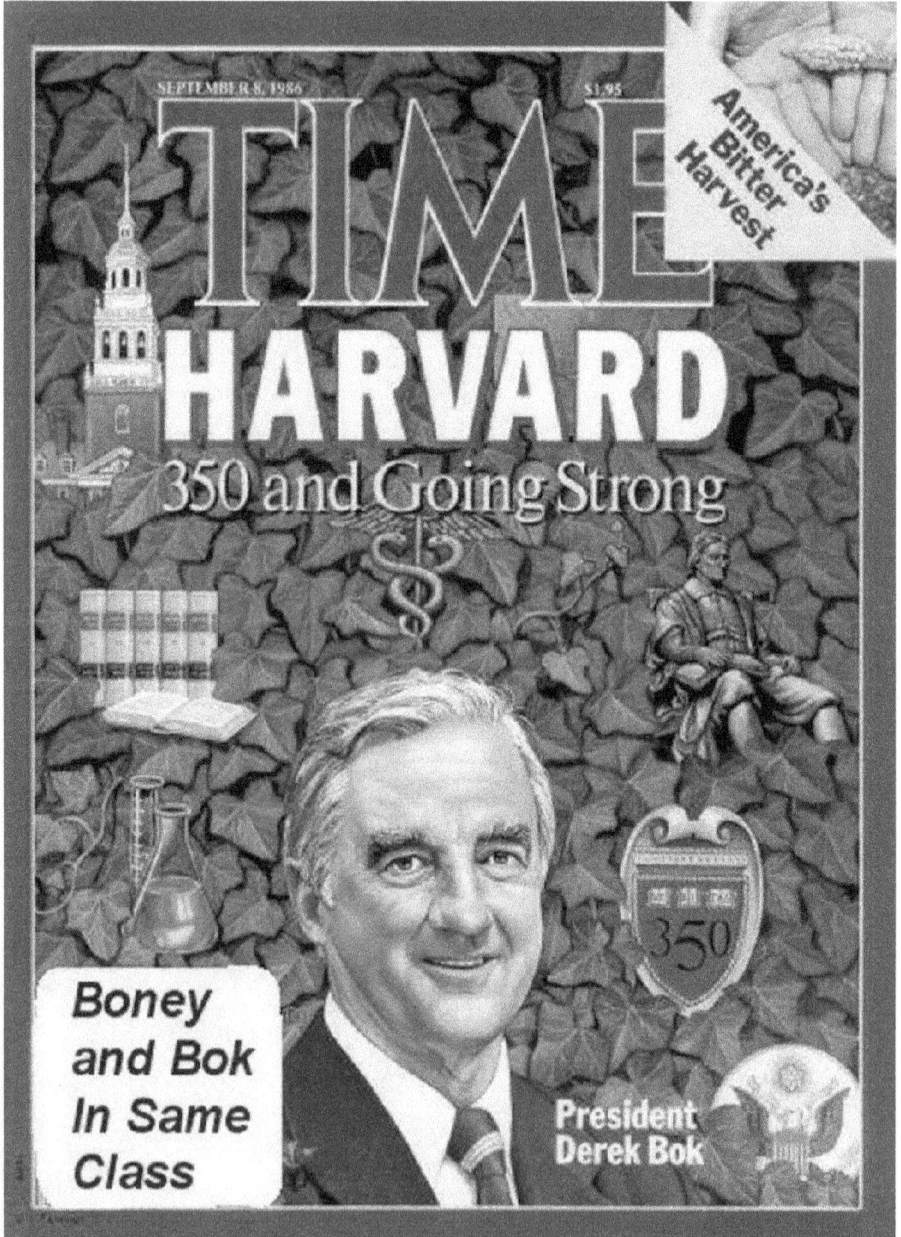

Part 41
Boney Clan, Fish Fry And Coach Bowden At The Football Reunion

Traditions, as we said, hang on tenaciously in the South — like barbeques, turnip greens (with pepper sauce) and fish fries. And speaking about that, the Boneys had just invited me to come up the road to enjoy a fish fry! You just cannot beat that kind of luck! And I had never eaten grits as good as they had there last Saturday. It was a scrumptious dinner prepared just past high noon; calling it a "lunch" would not adequately describe it. It was a full-blown dinner.

As I motored to Jacksonville and turned left toward China Hill I thought of the Boneys and George F. Boney who had reached a pinnacle in his brief career — becoming, at that time, the youngest Chief Justice of a state supreme court. In his case, it was Alaska.

As I continued driving I looked to my left as I approached Bethel Methodist Church and I could see his grave in the cemetery. It read 1930-1972. As I thought about that shining and brief moment of his I wondered about his personality and the kind of person he was. I would have liked to have known him.

I believe he had fun, with his serious responsibilities, because he had a Camaro. If you do not know what a Camaro is, I submit a picture so you can see a neat car. A friend of his, Ron Dolchok, said it was a 1967 beige automatic Camaro. Ron liked to drive the car when he got a chance.

When I arrived at Kyle Barron's beautiful home I met Tom Boney, a brother of George Boney. Tom, like George, did not let time go a-wasting. Tom is a gentleman and always wants to know about others. But I found that he has a passionate liking for real estate and has done pretty well down in Jacksonville, FL, at that. Previously he was the Director of Recreation and Public Affairs and handled the Gator Bowl, the Coliseum and other sport venues. Even the Zoo. He was busy - still is. He played for Coach Bobby Bowden at South Georgia College and they would be able to see each other at the weekend's reunion.

I also met Howell Boney, another brother of George Boney. He was also a busy man. He coached high school football in Jacksonville, FL, and was later the Director of Transportation for the Duval County Schools. Earlier, he had "walked on" at the University of Florida and told them he wanted to play football. At only about 5'5" or maybe a tad taller, only 175 pounds, he was to prove his mettle and spunk. As Georgia was beating Florida the Gator student body started chanting for their 3rd team guard Howell Boney — "We want Boney! We want Boney!" Boney was inserted. He upended at least three crucial plays, turned a lopsided score around and Florida won! From there on Howell Boney was a first team guard. Not only that, Howell Boney was awarded the GA-FLA Hall of Fame induction as its only representative in the position of guard.

Later at Douglas I enjoyed seeing these football players as they talked with FSU Coach Bobby Bowden and others. Coach Bowden, like the Boneys, had also reached a pinnacle. It is good to see folks succeed in what they like. It is also good to see others benefit from those folks who contribute so much. I appreciate FSU Coach Bowden for coming back to Douglas and renewing bonds and friendships. It says a lot for greatness. It says a lot about giving and not always getting.

It's just good to see folks doing something because they just want to do it. I am glad folks are like that — like Coach Bobby Bowden coming home for a reunion. And like LaJoy Boney who invited me to come to China Hill to eat fish and be with family. Just because they wanted to do it. You can't beat it.

Credit: Geri-Gadder Tours of Bainbridge, Ga.; our fellow travelers; KY, IA, MO, SD, WY, MT, Canada, AK info; Anchorage, AK; Tom Boney info on Justice George Boney; Howell Boney; Evelyn Boney Bramlitt; LaJoy Boney; Ron Dolchok; personal info; other sources.

We Enjoyed Alaska – But Russell Just About Killed Us! 159

Howell Boney
UF Florida Football
Hall of Fame

Julian Williams (Article)

Tom Boney
Played For
Coach
Bowden
At
SGC

Fish Fry Near China Hill 5-30-2009

Tom Boney Renews Football Days With Coach Bowden

Coach Bobby Bowden At SGC Reunion

Evelyn Boney Bramlitt Sister of Tom & Howell Boney

Justice Boney owned a beige 1967 Camaro. When colleagues wanted a ride he had to borrow a Buick.

Credit: Danny Whitfield

Part 42
Life Of Chief Justice Boney A Rich Legacy Of Brilliance, Common Sense And Love

"Life and death come to all
And in that space allowed
Our comings and goings
Toll the minuses and the pluses."

Linda Ellis, a poet, says it better:
*"So when your eulogy is being read
With your life's actions to rehash
Would you be proud of the things they say
About how you spent your dash?"*

Chief Justice George F. Boney of the Alaska Supreme Court, like all of us, then, now or later, have a "dash" (—) inserted between "born — died." George handled all that in superb fashion. George was a former Georgia person who was a responsible fellow. Florida, his later residence, would also affirm that. I think it had a lot to do with, as we said before, tradition. Later on we see that Alaska saw him in the same way.

It seems Boneys have always carried their tasks in a responsible way. By the time you read this, a young man near Jacksonville, Ga., will have received the highest honor — the Melvin Jones Award in Lionism — the Lions Club. Guy Durward Bland is a Boney on the maternal side. His mother was a Boney from China Hill, Ga. — the same Boneys we have been talking about for the last few weeks. I hope to be present for that presentation at Jacksonville, Ga., and witness the recognition Guy has so deservedly earned. To quote Lionism, "The fellowship is the foundation's highest honor and represents humanitarian qualities such as generosity, compassion, and concern for the less fortunate."

The last time I saw Guy was when we had the recent fish fry near China Hill and a lot of Boneys were around. That is the same time I stopped by the Bethel Cemetery and visited the grave of Chief Justice George F. Boney. Guy was a pallbearer for George's funeral. Guy and George — humanitarians. Both.

Others reflected on the life of Justice Boney. Even the Alaska's Governor Bill Egan, in fact, the first governor of the state, as it gained statehood in 1959, had a lot to say about Chief Justice Boney. And the Governor was reelected in 1970-74. Part of this time coincided with Boney's tenure at the high court. They worked together to make Alaska a better place.

Evidently, Governor Egan knew a lot about George Boney:

"Whether its origins lay in family upbringing, the regional rhythms of his Southern boyhood, or the law school he revered, George Boney was a man deeply moved by tradition. Tradition fortified his courage. Respect for scholarship gave temper to his craftsmanship. All these traits were sources to his deeply held commitment to individual freedom. Though his life was tragically short, George F. Boney has thus made his mark for we are all better off for his having fought the good fight."

Governor Egan and Chief Justice Boney were alike in their humanitarian bent. Egan liked to campaign and be with people. A humorous remark, but true, came from Egan when a correspondent told him he should be in first class on the airplane. "Yes," Egan replied, "but the voters are back here (second class)."

Tom Boney, brother of Justice Boney, made me think of George. As Tom was taking George on a tour of a facility in Jacksonville, Florida, Tom missed George. Looking for him he found him. He was talking to the workers outside and they were all having a good time conversing and enjoying themselves. George always had time to talk to people.

You almost had to go to Alaska to begin to get a small inkling (vague idea, not understanding) of the gigantic task of government, the vast expanse, the varied peoples, the cultures, the economics and the justice/courts of the land and the inhabitants. It was overwhelming to even think about all that. Violence, drug problems, victims and offenders of native folks being unable to communicate with others. And unable to understand each others' cultures. And on and on.

But Egan and Boney and others "buckled up" and tried to make Alaska a better place. In the hinterlands — remote locations — forgotten places, Justice Boney improved "bush justice." And he made the courts better in Anchorage. And Gov. Egan noted this (at George's funeral ceremonies):

*"This afternoon I noted the fine construction progress on the new state court building downtown and I couldn't help but think of the great enthusiasm and the work that Chief Justice Boney put in toward that day when the first earth was turned to begin the construction of that building. I think that it is fitting tonight for me to tell you that when that construction is finished that the dedicated building will be known as the Justice Boney Building (*Boney Courthouse*)."*

George's family, Stella (wife) and children, Frank, Jr., Cathy and Angela heard many colleagues speak well of George. He had died August 30, 1972, as a result of a sailboat accident at Cheri Lake, Houston, Alaska. But he filled much life in a short time (1930-1972). His dash (—) was full and fruitful.

As I finished the Justice George Boney sections I had the fortunate experience of hearing from one of daughters of Justice Boney — Angela Boney Frost. Of course, I could not leave out this information because it could be told only as an immediate family member. Luckily, Angela shared with me some of those rich nuggets of George's warm, magnanimous and unique personality.

From Angela I found that George Boney was his "own" man; even some considered him an unusual man; others might even label him an eccentric. George Boney knew what was important and he was able to divide the wheat from the chaff (tares). In other words, he knew the difference in good and bad, positive and negative, warmth and cold, achievement and making motions, realness and moot fodder, wisdom and foolishness, justice and injustice. He also knew the sagacity of not trying to strain a gnat to swallow a camel. Although he was an emotional man he also permitted this emotion to be tendered with stability and wisdom and discretion. He was a man's man (take a stand) but he was also the protector of the weak, the oppressed and the children. They could not have thought of a better title for George than "justice." He loved justice and it was a passion and he hated injustice and fought it to the end. He intended to fight for those who were not able to fight their own battles.

In fact, George would weep if he felt strongly about an issue or was very sad. Because of this strong but stable and expressive emotion he gained from worthy peers great respect and support. People liked George for being George and they knew when the battle had been fought and the smoke had cleared George would be around for accountability!

And Angela is quite a person, too. She has seven children and she and her husband are hoping to adopt an Asian girl baby. I suspect that in this progenitor/progeny fusing of George/Angela there is an exhibiting of these dominant traits that guides the family appropriately. And the Boney ancestors have practiced these good traits for a good while. Some of those old Boney ancestors were weathering Indian uprisings, battles and wars, piloting a ferry across Ocmulgee River, taking care of the sick, deciding hard situations, teaching their descendants and living in bad and good days — always trusting in God.

Angela relates that their dad was a very social man and loved people. It is not surprising to find that people loved him also. I found the same thing about the Boneys at China Hill. They were always wanting to be involved with governmental and civic affairs. At the same time they liked horses and hunting and fishing (and fish fries!) and having a good time. But like George, the other Boneys worked hard at whatever they were about. I always liked to work at the voting precinct at election time with Mr. Durward Boney because I felt he wanted to do the right thing. And he wanted everyone else to do the right thing, too! And, to boot, Durward Boney was also a football player — he was the quarterback at Fitzgerald High School in the 1920s. Angela's recollection of George included those same strong convictions - justice, a strong justice. Like other Boneys, George, according to Angela, could be very upset over injustice. I can understand how George Boney and the position of Chief Justice of Alaska were heading for an inevitable propitious (and fortunate) collision!

It is also not surprising that George liked work and was very passionate about his work. Work seems to work like this — everyone needs a basic reasonable paycheck to pay the bills. But beyond that, work becomes the pride of a person. Work becomes its creation and reflection and what the person stands for and the resulting workmanship. The person and the work are merged and melded and to talk about one or the other you have to talk about both. Unfortunately, some people never understand that principle and guiding light. George could see that light. And others could see it too. That ethic, in enough people, has sustained America.

By any measurement, George was not a cookie-cutter. In other words, he did not come out of a "normal" mold. Anything but it. He loved to get to his work — and work his brain - and work with people — but he was not overly concerned with which shirt appeared on his body or something called "acceptable attire." Angela said her mom worked hard to "suit him up" for work but after about five minutes he would have done away with that effort; and without trying, any clue of neatness was gone; again, he looked his own ruffled self! Like he had slept in his suit all night! And weekends it got worse, even intentionally, as he would dress sloppy and not shave. That was much more comfortable for going to their cabin and swimming in the lake. George was for making progress and enjoying life, not impressing anyone with him at any given time. He did it his way!

George liked to stay in shape but he was not below whipping up his great potato salad. And while he graciously shared this favorite he also ate quite copiously of same. So he gained a little weight. So he would diet some. Things would balance out!

Angela said, *"My dad was a genius with politics and the world situation. He always watched the evening news and always knew what was happening around the world. On the other hand he couldn't do handy man chores around the house. He wasn't very mechanical. Socially he was a little naive. People would sometimes joke at his expense and he didn't notice it. He was happy and jolly most of the time."*

As I read this passage I thought about similarities and differences in individual humans. Isn't it great that we are not the same! It would not be good to have all folks doing brain surgery and it would not be good having all folks picking up garbage — both very essential! It is good we all do different things and have different abilities, talents and gifts. Otherwise, it would be a boring world! Besides that, nothing would work out right!

Angela told me that her mom always helped George ride out cold winters as he felt somewhat depressed because he loved summers. George probably never got the warmth of Georgia and Florida out of his system. He did not welcome Alaska's "cold freezer." He liked warm weather; he did not like cold weather. He wore his long johns under his suit and wore this attire while at the office.

On the ski slope and practicing that exercise of skiing he must have struck others as someone who could "take it or leave," but liked to be up there for the social aspect — seeing and talking with everyone. But Angela remembered her daddy teaching her to ski when she was only four years old. Angela remarked that "the hill looked very steep to me." But I'll bet her daddy looked bigger and greater than the highest mountain. She remembers still — the good times. And if I am right, George Boney made a great effort in making it "the good times" for Angela and his family members.

To close this exchange with Angela I will not attempt to translate what she says about George Boney:

"He was a great provider and made sure that all of us were taken care of even if he were to die, which he didn't want to talk about. He would buy my mom pretty clothes when he went on business trips. He would just go into the ladies department of a fine store and ask the sales clerk to pick out something. It worked quite well. The sales clerk always had good taste. When my mom and dad would be at a dance, my dad would round up men for my mom to dance with since he didn't have good rhythm and my mom loved to dance. At church my dad would be singing the loudest but he was tone deaf. He didn't know that, he just thought if he knew the words he was good to go. It's a good thing that our Heavenly Father is pleased whether we hit the notes or not. He loved his family very much and he loved children. He was always kind to me. I have a lot of memories of my dad, so if you ever want to talk on the phone we can set up a time to do that. Well I must get back to the life of mother. Take Care and Aloha, Angela"

I hope Angela will write the whole book of Justice George Boney. I laughed as Angela told me about one of George's failures. We all make those — if we do anything! It seems that George was not interested in what was going on in his sixth grade. The teacher flunked him and sent him back a grade. But his "grit" was already in his constitution. He decided he would just show that teacher and all who were interested in his activities — that he could excel. From that point he began to accumulate "A" marks. He was an honor student in high school and college and on to law school. His intellectual abilities are well recorded and evident. He, for sure, was a different scholar and individual!

Yes, Angela, take care and Aloha. Thanks for sharing with us your daddy, George Boney. We are all better because we know a little more about this giant. Remember — write the book!

Credit: Geri-Gadder Tours of Bainbridge, Ga.; our fellow travelers; KY, IA, MO, SD, WY, MT, Canada, AK info; Anchorage, AK; Tom Boney info on Justice George Boney; Gov. Bill Egan; Guy Durward Bland; Linda Ellis; M.D. Kincaid; personal info; other sources.

Four Images Of George F. Boney
Thanks For Angela Boney Frost

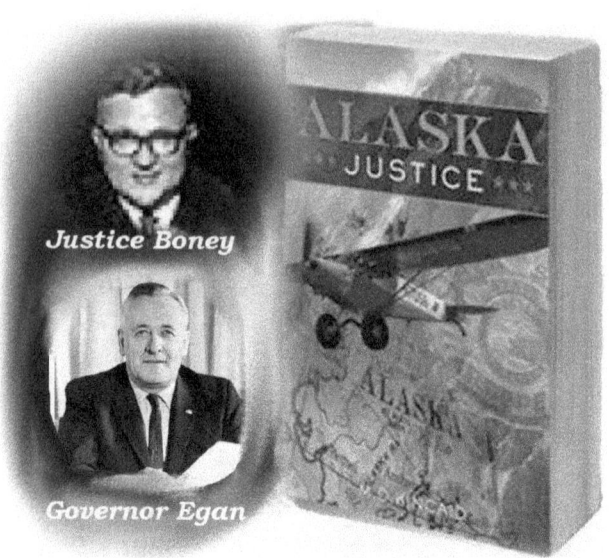

Justice Boney
Governor Egan
ALASKA
JUSTICE
ALASKA

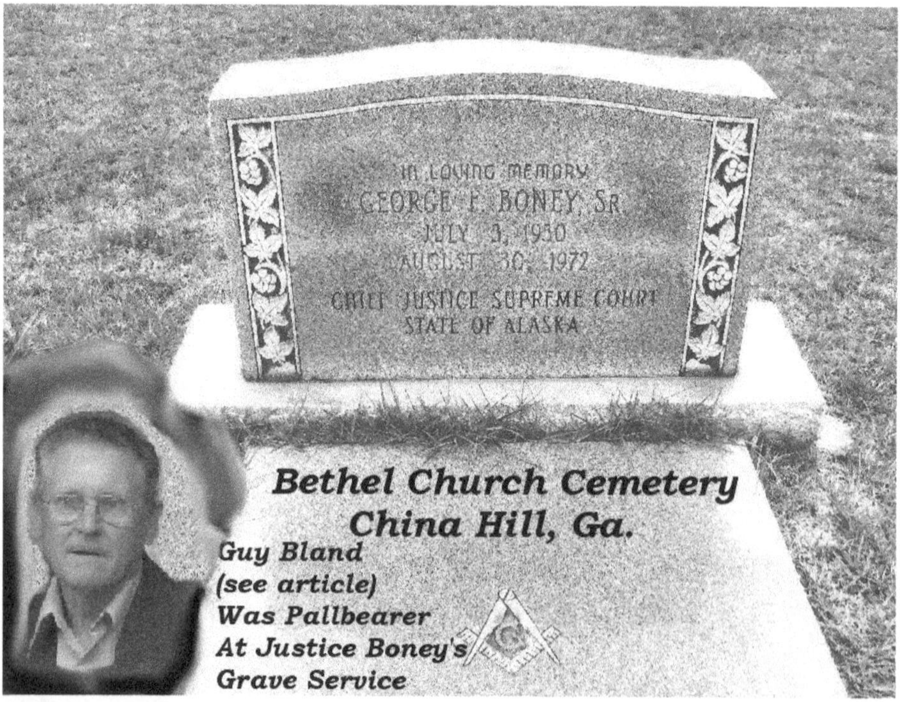
IN LOVING MEMORY
GEORGE F. BONEY, SR
JULY 3, 1930
AUGUST 30, 1972
CHIEF JUSTICE SUPREME COURT
STATE OF ALASKA
Bethel Church Cemetery
China Hill, Ga.
Guy Bland
(see article)
Was Pallbearer
At Justice Boney's
Grave Service

Part 43
An "Old Geezer" Alaskan Taught Engineers How To Build A Road

Leaving Anchorage, Alaska, we were glad to have had the opportunity of seeing the Boney Courthouse and some of the life of Chief Justice George F. Boney. We were also glad Mr. Boney left such a rich legacy. I suppose folks will continue to view his grave at little Bethel Methodist Church Cemetery at China Hill, Ga., just a few miles west of Jacksonville, Ga. Maybe these past articles will help viewers understand how George made such a remarkable circuit in his illustrious but short life.

Since we have already covered the wildlife park, Fairbanks, big cabbages, the native village and the North Pole, we will head for the end of the Alaska (Alcan) Highway at Delta Junction. Like many sleepy towns, Delta Junction, also ditto Fairbanks, sprang to life as World War II went full force. And to keep the momentum, here came the oil and the pipeline and things were humming.

But the older men, especially the older native men, knew a lot about dirt not known to the military. As these novice US soldiers converged on the primitive lands of Alaska they were determined to carry out orders of Washington, D.C. — build a road — and quickly. This was needed to help allies and thwart the Japanese attacks. The soldiers jumped quickly to do the road! On one section, an old timer grimaced and gestured to the young army leader that he could not put a road in that spot. The impatient officer replied to him that he would indeed put a road there. The native tried to make him understand why he could not do that. Ears were not listened. Closed conversation. Go on with the road!

As the days got hotter the permafrost began to give way and before you could do anything the whole big bulldozer had disappeared — swallowed beneath the new road! The young officer of course came unglued and frantically asked the old native if he could help. Yes. The old man showed the men how to design a stout harness, with leverage, and the location to stand with other machines — where the ground was solid. Slowly the procedure brought the bulldozer out of the mire and it was rescued. From then on the officer made the old native his right hand man and a road would only be placed where the old man instructed. Some of these old "geezers" are pretty smart!

Another site on this trip was interesting became it was an excellent sampling of "junk." Alaskans just don't throw away "junk." It might have a part or parts that would be necessary for them. In some instances keeping a part could mean the difference of living or dying! Alaska needs that machine owned by Jay Leno, TV entertainer. He likes cars and equipment and Jay has a scanner and a copier that can clone a part! He recently put in a Crescent wrench and in a little while out comes one just like it — and working! He can even copy a left handle, reverse the image in the computer, and come up with a right handle! What is the world coming to? Alaska would like to have that machine!

But even Alaska has its limits on "junk." I saw one couple who was warned about the excessive junk. His legal costs for the government is already over $200,000. I believe I would get rid of some of that junk!

And now it is getting a little later and the giant mosquitoes are hovering! We could not believe the size of those Alaskan mosquitoes! Someone asked me if many get on you. Half jesting I told him only one mosquito would fit on your arm! I show you a picture of some of those mosquitoes. Of course, these mosquitoes are a little bigger than real mosquitoes — but not much! When Russell saw the size of those mosquitoes he would not come out of the bus!

Credit: Geri-Gadder Tours of Bainbridge, Ga.; our fellow travelers; KY, IA, MO, SD, WY, MT, Canada, AK info; Delta Junction, AK; other sites; personal info; other sources.

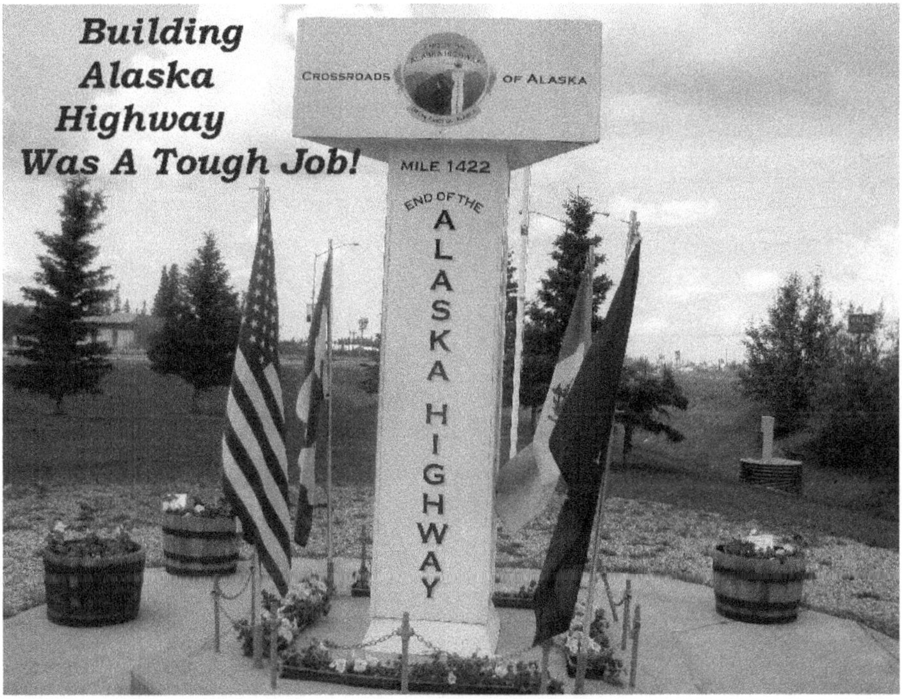
Building
Alaska
Highway
Was A Tough Job!
CROSSROADS
OF ALASKA
MILE 1422
END OF THE
ALASKA
HIGHWAY

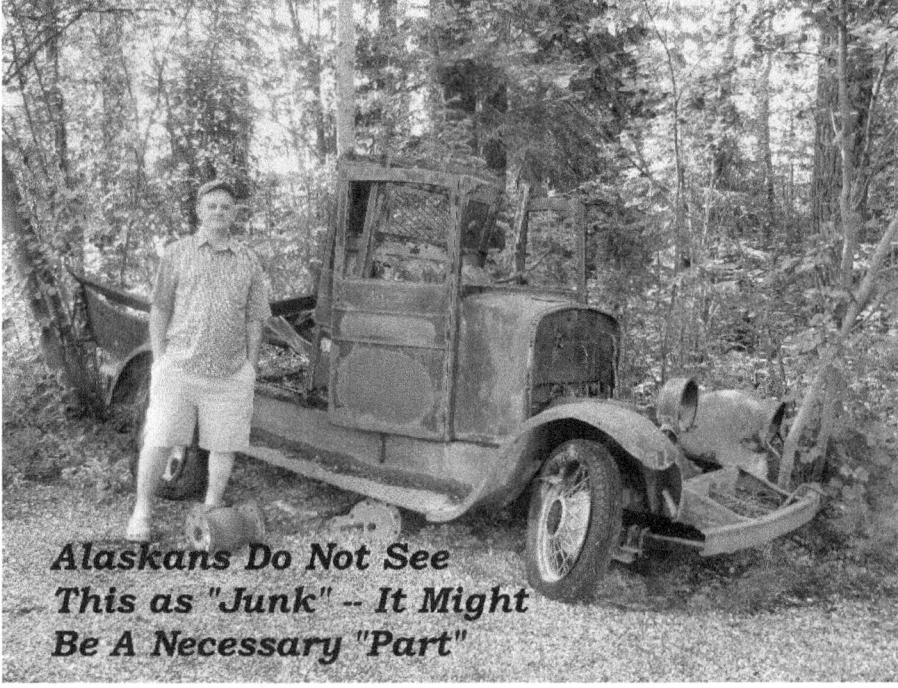

Alaskans Do Not See
This as "Junk" -- It Might
Be A Necessary "Part"

Part 44
Monstrous Mosquitoes
And Lawn Mowers On The Roofs

I hope our ladies visiting the "washroom" in Alaska (restroom) are not unfairly plagued by those eternal infernal mosquitoes. But due to a human female physical makeup it is more difficult to move quickly, versus men, to evacuate a toilet. Also, ironically, female mosquitoes are the biting offenders. It seems, according to our guides, that the female mosquitoes have to get blood to assimilate other fluids with their ovaries so their eggs will develop. These searching little Draculas zero on you if you are in the scope. But don't feel like you are anyway superior for this plasma; in fact, bloodsucker mosquitoes prefer pulling blood from cows and goats rather than humans. While all these violent female mosquitoes are doing harm to warm-blooded creatures the male mosquitoes are leisurely sipping at flowers and extracting sugary nectars. It was hard to believe this pecking order placed humans low-totem-pole while my fleeing frame was trying to outrun those buzzing female eviscerators. Also, I suppose you would have to pair up with a cow and a bell to cause a diversion to avoid being swamped by those mosquito hellions. So, come to Alaska, and see the real deals! You will appreciate Georgia!

It seems we picked just the right time to come to Alaska — June/July. So if you want the same privileges be sure to go to Alaska in the summer. This way you will be sure, like us, to be deboned and blood-transfused by those renowned super mosquitoes. One quipster said those mosquitoes were so huge the air traffic controllers had to clear them for landing and taking off! You can also pick from quite a selection as there are about 35-40 varieties of these mosquitoes. But I could not guarantee you can get any small bugs in all this array.

After those monstrous mosquitoes finished a meal of my body I was ready to seek the refuge of our bus where Russell was tightly and silently ensconced — securely in one of the back seats. However, Russell does not weigh too much and it is within possibilities that those flying pests might well fly off with Russell. I figure those mosquitoes can fly off with Russell if they can disable an Alaskan caribou and take it away. Thinking about it, just before getting into the bus, I swatted a swarming bunch of those pesky things and killed eight. But that was nothing, one man claims he killed 64 at one lick! Good for him!

But, truth told, the Ocmulgee River swamp is no slouch when it comes to active robust mosquitoes. They also hurt! I say that not to take away the recognition and supremacy of Alaska but to say that I have never seen a friendly mosquito.

But, we had a lot of time to be on the lookout for mosquitoes because darkness hardly came. In Alaska you have a lot of daylight in the summer — like 18 or 20 hours! You had to close your curtains in the hotel to get to sleep.

You also better get ear plugs aplenty! Here we are trying to sleep and at about 2:30 a.m. some soul cranks up the nearby lawn mower! Now, we are up on the second story so normally this height would render the noise negligible. But not in our situation: the lawn mower is not on the ground as you would normally think. The lawn mower is on the roof of the house — exactly across from our second story room. Believe it or not, some folks grow grass on the roof! Why, I don't know — unless it forms insulation or maybe distracts the mosquitoes! Cranking up! Varoom! — jet 'um — butt 'um — tide 'em — putt, putt, putt — and all the different noises a lawn mower (without muffler) can make! Maybe he couldn't find "a part."

But those good folks think nothing of these routines because that is a great time for cutting the grass — when they get off the "night shift" which is really a second or third "daylight shift."

Now fully awake I walk across the room and open the curtains and peer out the window. Resignedly, I smiled weakly as I put up an arm to welcome the lawn worker and let him know that Alaska reigns in that domain.

I felt good because the lawn mower man raised his arm. I just knew that he was returning my salutation. But, alas, I was not correct in projecting such an exchange of greetings. The man was just raising his arm to flail the daylights out of another bad mosquito.

As I tried to get a little more sleep I thought of the jokester who said he was nominating an Alaskan mosquito to replace the state bird, the ptarmigan. Really makes sense — at least it was easier to say and spell! And lots more aggressive and expressive!

We Enjoyed Alaska – But Russell Just About Killed Us! 175

The long Alaskan days were endless — and so our days from distant Georgia. Russell was ready to call a screeching halt to all this foolishness. We were headed in that direction! But, give me more of that DEET for these mosquitoes! And don't get it on the camera case; it will melt it!

Credit: Geri-Gadder Tours of Bainbridge, Ga.; our fellow travelers; KY, IA, MO, SD, WY, MT, Canada, AK info; Delta Junction, AK; other sites; personal info; other sources.

Down in the Ocmulgee Swamp we fought mosquitoes and looked for an old Spanish Mission - and other things.
~~ Julian Williams

Lawn Mower On Top Of The House

Part 45
Picnic, Hot Springs And Walls
Of Old Car Tags From Everywhere

Swimming in Alaska and Canada was something some of our fellow travelers could not resist. In fact, a friend John Milhous was in the water just about every time you looked around. John Milhous loves to swim. It is good exercise and is relaxing.

Some of us did not take our swim trunks to Alaska/Canada and if we did we didn't go swimming. After visiting the Liard Hot Springs east of Watson Lake, Canada, I wished I was in there. But it was enjoyable just seeing John in the hot springs. John was such an advocate and enthusiast for swimming he could tell you what place we would be visiting next and whether it had a swimming pool or not!

If you ever go there to Liard you will find a beautiful place and everything is not primed up and painted like some commercial swimming pool. The springs were kept much as the original layout. Of course, there is a boardwalk and some wooden railings for getting in and out of the springs and protection. Beyond that the springs are just like nature left them.

After getting our picture taken by the hot springs we followed the trail back to our bus where restrooms and picnic tables were available. Our tour director advised us to take snacks along as no stores would be there in the wild. He was right.

Later we were introduced to some disturbing history about the hot springs. The good news was that I did not know at that date that big black bears appeared in this location. The bad news was that a big black bear killed two tourists there a few years back.

But we were always ready to eat. Out of our paper sacks came canned meats, chips, pudding cups and assorted cold drinks, etc. Russell always stays up toward the head of the table so he can keep an eye on all the rest of us. We cannot eat until Russell gives thanks for our food and we are glad he keeps us straight on that. That is probably the most important thing we do — to give God our thanks and praises

— for everything — not just the food.

But, even this nice location brought back quick negative stimulation to Russell as he remembered the nearby place called Sign Post Forest. Here were thousands of state and province tags placed there by people far and near. About sixty thousand tags were displayed. Unbelievable! Someone said a homesick soldier from Illinois placed the first one in 1942.

As Russell started looking over this vast array of tags he found several "Georgia" tags. His mind immediately started churning out his desires — "Georgia, Georgia — Georgia on my mind." We took a picture of a small sample of those tags. We put the tag "Lowndes County, Ga." in an inset in the picture. We could not find one for Coffee or Telfair. Russell's sentiments were that he did not need a tag to remember the event. He was here and that was bad enough! His radar on his scope was getting larger and larger and all he could see was "Georgia."

But the scenery at Watson Lake was great. We enjoyed the boardwalk from the springs and we enjoyed our picnic with our friends J.L. and Doris Sutton of Dahlonega, Ga. And I was glad I didn't know about the big black bear at the time. I would have walked faster on the boardwalk and eaten faster at the picnic. Alaska and Canada have scenarios of mixed emotions. Good and bad. Russell agreed — but to him it was mostly bad!

Credit: Geri-Gadder Tours of Bainbridge, Ga.; our fellow travelers; KY, IA, MO, SD, WY, MT, Canada, AK info; Watson Lake, Canada; other sites; personal info; other sources.

Picnic Near Liard Hot Springs, Canada

Russell, Grace, Doris, J.L., Julian, Joanne

Liard Hot Springs

Julian, Joanne, Grace, Russell

Part 46
Bigfoot And Canada's Sasquatch And A Similar Booger At Jacksonville, Georgia

Somebody mentioned "Bigfoot." A slightly nervous aura in our midst told me something was a little different. I even started itching — like big hairs were drifting down my collar. My skin was getting clammy. Folks began to crane their necks to see what was up the road. Earlier we had heard of a very strange creature as our bus was traversing the areas of western Canada. Here they called him "Sasquatch." Maybe more than one. We were getting closer to location "X."

And, we had already been unnerved at an earlier site with news of a deadly black bear. But this next creature was even more fearful and foreboding than the prospects of a large bear. And we were getting very near to the location of this habitat of this terrible beast. I could tell quickly that Russell did not hanker to encounter this dreadful species. To make Russell feel better I started telling him what I knew of such beasts in Georgia.

My experience many years ago of such beasts was gained at Old Jacksonville, Georgia. For many weeks reigned a tentative anxiety as some unknown creature (or creatures) was/were stomping along, or stalking, across the expanses of the Ocmulgee River swamps. They said when the creature picked up his feet, deep in the mire, because he was so heavy, an ominous sucking sound resulted. Enough to scare anyone.

Reports began revealing big shadowy outlines moving with great swiftness, grunting unintelligible speech, and stamping the very indelible prints deep into the mud of those huge feet! It was just the thing to motivate the local inhabitants into apt attention around Jacksonville, Ga. Comfort and satisfaction got into a new gear; a brisk step picked up the slack.

It was beginning to get worse than when the Civil War Yankees swooped down and terrorized the river road citizenry by acting disorderly and disrespectful, stealing (taking) everything that was not secreted beneath the yard or hidden in the woods. But with the Yankees they could be identified. It was not that easy with this new creature.

But the folks, maybe not quite armed with the reputation, credentials and expertise of Sherlock Holmes, were determined to find out what was going on in the swamps. Besides that, the babies and the children could not sleep comfortably and carry on with their chores. The booger out there had to be found and eradicated.

But the great manhunt, or search, hardly got off running, even walking, until some local sleuth came up with the mystery. He discovered a pair of very large plywood "feet" that had been cleverly attached to a normal (give or take a little) fellow who masqueraded the night specter and scared the daylights out of some of the neighbors. But at least the guilty schemer had caused some excitement. It's a wonder that the Telfair Enterprise had not become a daily newspaper. To see the probable "Jacksonville booger" see the attached photo.

But, back in Canada, Russell and I peeled our eyes lest we be surprised. Sasquatch might be looking at you!

But the good old boys got a good laugh just like Jacksonville, Ga., got years ago. The only Sasquatch on this store corner was a man (or woman) with a costume. But I would have hated to run into that thing in a dark alley.

Pictures were taken and Russell was getting braver each day. He even said the big black bear at his table would have to share his table - or else!

Credit: Geri-Gadder Tours of Bainbridge, Ga.; our fellow travelers; KY, IA, MO, SD, WY, MT, Canada, AK info; somewhere in "Sasquatch" territory in Canada; unknown person of the picture of the bear at the table; other sites; personal info; other sources.

We Enjoyed Alaska – But Russell Just About Killed Us!

Russell told me to be sure to label the ones in the picture.

Grace   Sasquatch   Russell
(Yes, I was tempted!)

Looked Just Like "Bigfoot" Near Jacksonville, Ga.

Part 47
Big Hay Fields, John Deere, Chuckwagons And Rolling Stores

Our bus was zooming along and we enjoyed the vast fields around us. It seemed like for miles we could see golden hay rolled up and displayed on the seemingly limitless acreage spread before our view. The distant horizon seemed to dissolve with hay fields into a pale yellowish-bluish sky. Somebody was going to have to have some know-how manpower and great pieces of machinery to get all this hay to the barn. And what a barn it must be! I thought we had some big fields in Coffee County and Telfair County in Georgia but those were little patches compared to those Canadian expanses.

And just about when Russell and I were marveling about the magnitude of all this agriculture and land we stopped at a pioneer park that reflected and contained some of these farm machines and other interesting things. In fact, there were some of the John Deere products. I had not really thought about John Deere being a man. I always, for some unknown notion, thought a John Deere was a tractor. Seeing a portrait of the man, John Deere, was a treat. So, I figured, this is the man who started all those tractors.

Well, yes and no. John Deere started off in his father's tailor shop and ended up being the best man around for inventing and building plows. In the past his tailor shop experiences taught him that he could sharpen needles with sand. Employing this knowledge allowed him to make the best polished steel plows in the prairie. His new plow would not clog up with the clay and would work well in this situation.

Interestingly, John Deere never made a tractor. But his work before that development helped others build tractors. His company, The John Deere Company, soon was a top contender with tractor design and production.

As I looked at the portrait of John Deere I thought about those vast hay fields. Even though I appreciated Mr. Deere and those big fields I still wondered how they were able to get lunch to "hands" working in the fields. My goodness — it would take a truck and a tank of gas and half the day, or more, to get around! But someone figured all that out too! Here attached is a picture of a chuckwagon — a rolling wagon equipped with a kitchen. The chuckwagon went with the workers and when it was time to eat their lunch was ready.

When I looked at this chuckwagon I thought of Old Jacksonville, Ga., and a few connected memories. We didn't have a chuckwagon but we had a rolling store and the rolling store just like the chuckwagon was there when you needed it. If it was not there just that moment it would not be long coming down the road. If you didn't have cold cash you could swap (barter) a dozen eggs or a chicken for some cloth or sugar or a pot or a pan or a bottle of eye medicine or something else. The other thing connected to "chuckwagon" was my favorite gospel group, "The Chuck Wagon Gang." The old radio would bring you those singers each day if you could find the time to tune in at 12:45; I tried to make my dinner (lunch) coincide with that great event.

But, the mention of eye medicine got Russell going. When he got back from Alaska and Canada he said he was going to see a doctor about doing something about his eyes. But Russell informed me that he could see all he wanted to or needed to in Alaska or Canada. He was ready to get to Georgia!

Credit: Geri-Gadder Tours of Bainbridge, Ga.; our fellow travelers; KY, IA, MO, SD, WY, MT, Canada, AK info; a pioneer park of exhibits in Canada; other sites; personal info; other sources.

Chuckwagon in Canada
(see attached article)

Part 48
Big Canada Mall, An Old Stove And A Sweet Memory Of Grandmama's Stewed Tomatoes

I bet our Valdosta friend, John Milhous, would like to get in that swimming pool at Edmonton, Canada. I suppose that pool is the biggest I ever saw. Someone said there are five acres in it! Looking at the picture you can see that it appeared about half of the folks of the city must be in the pool! A couple of slides in the pool were over seventy feet high. I don't know if John got in there but I tell you one thing — if he got just a little chance he was in there. I started to ask Barbara if John had scales; but I bet he is in good shape with all that swimming. Our seats were just behind Barbara and John and we enjoyed being with them. They can also guide you to some good eating places around Thomasville and Valdosta and we look forward to getting to one of those towns and again breaking bread with them.

The whole place (Canadian mall) was pretty impressive if you looked at bigness. The mall was for a long time the largest in the world. Of course, everybody tries to beat that but I think it is now the largest inside mall in North America. Our ladies went wild in the place. You could find about anything in those stores. I looked up some information and it said over 23,000 people were employed in that mall. I was glad there was no room in the bus to put shopping bags.

But we finally rounded up everyone and were heading up the road. Coming into one of the pioneer parks we saw an old wood stove. I show you that old stove (picture) and I hope it will also remind you of pleasant memories. It certainly caused me to smile.

My Grandmother Effie Williams at Jacksonville, Georgia, had a stove similar to that. She could cook anything but my favorite was stewed tomatoes with milk and sugar. Of course, butter and salt and pepper were included. I have found that recipe almost extinct now but I have played with those ingredients until I have just about gotten close to Grandma's specialty. Well, I had better take that back — or I might be lying! Nobody could cook that concoction like Grandmother Effie

Williams. I also make a substitution for the sugar. I pour in about four Sweet'n Low packets but that simmering soup is still mighty good. You should try it. Chip up a biscuit or two and put it in there and you have something you will want to write or phone relatives and friends!

When I was a little boy I was in my special chair (really, a bench) at Grandmama's — eating my tomato stew with milk and sugar. A man visiting asked Grandmother if that was all I was going to eat — considering all the other fine food on the table. Grandmother smiled and said that would not be all that I would eat. In fact, Grandmother told him I would probably eat another big bowl of the same! And I did — with crumbled up biscuits in there.

As we left the old stove and the old tractors and the blacksmith tools and the old cars and buggies and the little churches and the schoolhouse with the bell and other things a person could really pack back a lot of memories right there. I remember one horse and buggy stayed right there all Saturday at a tree at Jacksonville, Ga., until the owner did his shopping, talked to neighbors and rolled a few Prince Albert cigarettes and finished his other business. This is a different day.

Pulling into another place our guide enthusiastically shouted, "Saskatoon, Saskatchewan!" We were entering the academy of the Canadian Mounties!

Russell looked a little anxious. He was probably thinking the Mounties would try to keep him north of the border. But Russell had a plan and you will see the picture that explains his intentions.

Credit: Geri-Gadder Tours of Bainbridge, Ga.; our fellow travelers; KY, IA, MO, SD, WY, MT, Canada, AK info; various sites and exhibits in Canada; personal info; other sources.

Part 49
Canada's Mounties Train
And Strive To Be The Best

As we skirted the skyline of Saskatoon, Saskatchewan, we admired the gilded gleaming buildings. The place is also known as the city's river of seven bridges. We had anxiously looked for the Mounties but we would have to wait a little to see the Royal Canadian Mounted Police Museum and Academy. It was just a little south — to Regina.

We caught a little nap on the bus and soon we were rolling into Regina. The entrance told us quickly that this was a serious place and the Mounties were not up to any foolishness. That was mostly true but some lighter fare was exhibited and permitted and we were even allowed to take pictures of fellow travelers posed with a "fun" cutout of a Mountie on a horse. The head was left vacant for a visitor to appear in the cutout. That is how Russell became a Mountie. His image appeared nearby. That item will probably be placed in some permanent archive so others can enjoy it.

But back to the serious side. I jumped right in the group with our leader who was going to take us to the Mounties and their drill field. You will see a picture here and can see that the raw recruits are beginning to shape into what will become full-fledged Mounties.

They tell me it takes six months for a recruit to earn his uniform and what it stands for. Through this mental and physical toughness these recruits undergo a lot of stress and strain. The Royal Canadian Mounted Police ordeal is compared to the training of a U.S. Marine recruit. That is tough. Just to think of coming up to that standard speaks well of the Mountie.

As we walked toward the drill field we saw something that stopped us. As Mounties' personnel walked by a certain monument they would face it and sharply salute it before passing by. Observing the monument closer we could see the names of Mounties killed in the line of duty. Above those names were flags and below an eternal flame.

This honor did not only dedicate and consecrate those who had fallen in duty; it also reminded the Mounties and/or the recruits that their standard must be high and noble. It also reminded them that they would carry out their assignments in peril and danger.

Near this was a yellow line. We were not allowed to cross that yellow line. It reminded us that certain things around there were sacred and costly. It reminded us that these young men and women were striving for a service that would be enviable but difficult. It reminded us that few would attain that status.

As we reached the chapel the sacred refuge revealed again the sacrifices of the The Force. We usually call them "Mounties" but the service call themselves "The Force." It is an apt label.

Recently, women were admitted as Mounties. On the drill field we saw women drilling with the men. As we moved to another point we witnessed some proud Mounties as they carried their "Stetsons" (hats) as they were graduating. Some of those were women. One of the top officers of the service is a woman. We have included a picture of a Mountie lady. Russell said he had rather face her than that one on the border!

As we studied these men and women we could see the determined countenance, the professional pride, the carriage of poise and courage and justice. We could understand a little of what it meant to be a Mountie.

Of Sergeant Preston it was said, "He always gets his man." And the way of getting him meant a lot to the Mountie. He would rather talk a man into surrendering than shoot him. That was the way of the Mountie. Class.

As we left the Museum and the Academy we will always remember the horses and the cannon and the firearms and the uniforms of scarlet, dark blue and gold and the tales of bravery and tenacity and resplendence. But what we will always remember about the Mounties — they strive to be "the best." A tradition that is hard to beat!

Credit: Geri-Gadder Tours of Bainbridge, Ga.; our fellow travelers; KY, IA, MO, SD, WY, MT, Canada, AK info; Kim Cauthen Hill for modeling lady Mountie; various sites and exhibits in Canada; personal info; other sources.

Part 50
Giant Paul Bunyan, "Dead-Ringers" And Some Pretty Big Men At Jacksonville, Georgia

As we leave beautiful Canada we now know we are headed homeward. Reaching the United States in North Dakota we stop at a little town called Rugby. At first we did not assign anything special to this little place but quickly found that Rugby is the geographical center of North America!

Before we knew it we were looking at a giant cairn (monument) proclaiming Rugby as the central point. Emphasizing their unique position Rugby flew proudly aloft the flags of Canada, United States and Mexico.

The place might have been the center of these three countries but it sure didn't look like a location for that distinguished designation. But we took pictures and place one here so you can see the picture also.

You can never tell about any particular town or city. Rugby also has a funeral home with a 30-foot tower containing 15 bells! These bells are not for "dead-ringers" to wake the dead (or, rather almost dead persons mistakenly placed in graves!) but to call the citizens for certain meetings, announcements, etc. The bells are quite historical as they come from old churches and schools. The whole production certainly speaks loudly for the community!

As we left this town I thought about "dead-ringers" again. My Granddaddy Anderson, a young pallbearer, noticed a "dead" man's eyelid quiver on the way to the cemetery. The "deceased" man was already in the pine box! When Granddaddy Anderson saw the movement again he called Dr. Brown who examined the man, massaged his heart and brought him out of the casket. He lived for another five years! Close to being a dead-ringer!

Russell was slightly smiling as we reached Wisconsin. His nose was oriented South and he knew if he followed the trail he would wind up in Georgia. It was hard to get him to turn around as that would point him toward the direction of north. He did not want to lose his trail.

And here we are — at another legend — Paul Bunyan! The great big log-cutter with his giant Babe Blue Ox was a sight! Paul and Babe were thought highly in the north woods. Their feats were legend and they did some unbelievable things! Like digging the Grand Canyon! We posed with one of these huge figures so you can see those too!

But the best part of Paul Bunyan was its namesake — a place called Cook Shanty. Now we evermore enjoyed a meal there. It was just about more than Paul could eat!

Pulling away on our bus I got to thinking about Paul Bunyan and all those tall tales. But we had some timber tales at Jacksonville, Georgia, that were absolutely true!

There was a log-cutter there called Big John and one day got killed under a falling tree. He and his buddies came from the Black Forest and probably were German POWs. But folks here liked these fellows as they were good timber workers. Mr. Jim Lowe at Jacksonville, Ga., did not have a casket for a six-foot, five-inch man. His buddies said they could just cut his legs off but the Lowes worked all night to come up with an appropriate casket that would fit Big John.

Uncle John Pruitt, Jacksonville, Ga., was also a legend. His fine-tuned, accurate bullwhip could pick a horsefly off an ox's ear — and ox or Uncle John did not miss a step!

It was said in Jacksonville, Ga., that a massively muscled woodsman lifted up a full barrel of tar and placed it on a wagon. Almost unbelievable. And almost good as Paul Bunyan!

A new place coming. What is this? A mouse or a cheese? Maybe both. And here we look at Grace and Joanne posing with the Mouse (in front of the nice cheese store)! And somehow I get the impression that Mastercard will be the impression!

Credit: Geri-Gadder Tours of Bainbridge, Ga.; our fellow travelers; KY, IA, MO, SD, WY, MT, Canada, AK, ND, WI; personal info; other sources.

Rugby, North Dakota Central Point of Canada, US, Mexico

The Tales Of Paul Bunyan Were Bigger Than Those Of Jacksonville, Ga.

Russell Grace Paul Joanne Julian

We Enjoyed Alaska – But Russell Just About Killed Us!

Grace   Cheese   Mouse   Joanne

Part 51
We Bid Farewell – Alaska And Canada
Our Fine Memories Are Overflowing

Finally we got Joanne and Grace out of that "cheese store" — so abundantly stocked with all kinds of goodies. Wisconsin folks have a knack of making something attractive and working hard at perfecting that objective.

But all was not well in Wisconsin. In just a little while we were in beautiful country but the rains had come — torrential rains and plenty of it. We passed a cemetery and this picture will attest to the great rains. Part of the cemetery was flooded and the graves and monuments were underwater or partially so. I thought about the Flint River at Albany, Ga. — where some caskets had actually risen and were floating down the river! I hope that did not happen to any Wisconsin bodies reposed in that cemetery.

Another place stopped us in our steps! The House on the Rock in Wisconsin is something that I cannot adequately describe. An architect named Alex Jordan was dismissed from the famous architect Frank Lloyd Wright who said, "I would not let you design a cheese crate or a chicken coop." To seek a playful revenge Jordan began to make his own house — and what a house! The house and all the furnishings reflected a monstrous parody of Wright.

The house goes on — rambling — to dens and attics and hallways and rooms and you seem to never get anywhere! One place is called the Infinity Room. Other creations are works of art, some refined, some grotesque and from all parts of the world. The whole thing is a piece of work and you could never see it all. And the son has taken over and continues to work on this colossal project. At last count some half a million persons each year visit this location at a clip of $15 per person. It is a place you will never forget. You might like it or not like it but you will remember it!

After that venue, I welcomed the remaining miles through the USA toward home! I smiled at Louisville, KY, as we saw the ball park; and thought of those Hillerich Louisville Slugger bats and how long ago we enjoyed those at Jacksonville, Ga., as we coveted those bats at our baseball field. And in another era I thought about the steamboats passing by Louisville from New Orleans and Pittsburgh. They had a long trip on rivers! And I thought about the old steamboats that left Macon, Ga., and wound up in Darien, via Jacksonville, Ga. That must have been a grand time in history.

Now we are getting closer and closer to home — Georgia — and the trip has been a fine one. But I think that I will never see anything as beautiful as Alaska and Canada. The land is nearly pristine and truly one of the last frontiers. It is also one — or at least a large portion — unmolested by civilization and free of pollutants and other undesirable byproducts. But accidents have shown its havoc in its undesirable results (spilled oil, etc.).

But people in Alaska and Canada can be proud to live in their domains — the falling streams, some spectacularly high and cascading; the panoramas of green foliage exhibiting every shade of green you can imagine; primitive animals still there, bison/buffalo and musk ox with the appearance of something long ago; lakes and ponds and rivers that run the gamut of colors, either tinged with minerals or left intact with the purity of hidden springs; the independence of the people, geared to survive in a wilderness and determined not only to survive but to excel; the character of the whole country, so exemplified by the Mounties and the Rangers; the resources so abundant in oil, gas and other precious gems and elements; the adventure and danger inherent in this land, as volcanoes threaten to change a city and population as quickly as an eruption happens; to sum it up, and it cannot be truly summed up, this land is different, it is sacred, it is beautiful, and it contains those things, living and non-living, that cannot be equaled. The native history of this land spans thousands and thousands of years and these natives are still there and living out and satisfying their wills and traditions and contributing to all.

Alaska! Canada! Long may you live and flourish! We will always keep a part of your hearts in our hearts and in times to come we will flip through our pictures and our memories and know again that we visited places to be envied - and cherished. Thanks for the trip!

Credit: Geri-Gadder Tours of Bainbridge, Ga.; our fellow travelers; KY, IA, MO, SD, WY, MT, Canada, AK, ND, WI, IL, IN, KY, TN, GA; personal info; other sources.

We Enjoyed Alaska – But Russell Just About Killed Us!